PARK LEARNING CENTRE
UNIVERSITY OF GLOUCESTERSHIRE
PO Box 220, The Park
Cheltenham GL50 2RH
Tel: 01242 714333

Online Business
Security Systems

Online Business Security Systems

by

Godfried B.Williams
University of East London
UK

Springer

Godfried B. Williams
School of Computing & Technology
University of East London
Docklands Campus
4-6 University way
London
E16 2RD
email.g.williams@uel.ac.uk

Library of Congress Control Number: 2007925870

Online Business Security Systems
by Godfried B. Williams

ISBN: 978-0-387-35771-3   e-ISBN: 978-0-387-68850-3

Printed on acid-free paper.

9 8 7 6 5 4 3 2 1

springer.com

Dedications

To my mother, Letitia, who is dear to my heart

In memory of my father, Godfried whom I carry his memory

To my wife, Sylvia, whose love for me is a fortress

To my gracious daughter, Maxine and son, Jordan
who bring joy to my heart

To my nephews and nieces who share my life

Contents

List of Figures

List of Tables

Foreword

Without question the topic of security is one of the most important subjects in today's information technology environment, if not the most important. As we have a foot in both the business and academic environments, we believe that it is imperative that advances in security be propagated from the realm of lofty ideas in our academic institutions into the real world. Security has always been an obvious concern in government environments, but is also a major concern to the business community. Defense from multiple threats is required to provide for the security of business assets both in the form of financial and information resources. Additionally these threats can come in the form of both internal and external attacks. All of the doors must be guarded.

As of the end of 2006 new regulations have been set in place within the United States that require a higher standard of electronic record keeping from all entities, both public and private. Similar standards are either in place or being considered world wide. These higher standards call for a higher level of security, both on internal company, governmental and educational networks as well as externally in the online world of the Internet. This online requirement applies to the Internet as a whole, and also to extranets and intranets, running over the world IP pipeline.

Dr. Williams has previously addressed some of these issues in his prior work, "Synchronizing E-Security," (2004). He has pointed out the major problem in security expenditures between advanced and developing economies that has resulted in a security gap that should be of concern to us all. Besides the obvious concern in today's dangerous world of overt terrorism that can be spread to electronic means, is the additional concern of fraud and theft that must be guarded against in all types and levels of institutions.

Dr. Williams's new book is a valuable addition towards the solution to these issues and problems to bring increased awareness of the issues, problems and potential solutions to create a safer environment in Online Business Security Systems. This work is a piece of that solution and hopefully more insights such as this one will follow, both from Dr. Williams and his peers in security research and development.

Don Anderson
President, Quantum International Corporation
Founding Member, Intellas Group, LLC

Adel Elmaghraby, Ph.D.
Chair
Department of Computer Engineering and Computer Science
University of Louisville, USA

Preface

According to empirical studies by Williams (2004), the paradox in security expenditure between advanced and developing economies has resulted in a security gap. The irony is that while investments in security amongst IT companies in advanced economies are not that high in budget, the methods employed for assessing possible risks in the application of technologies are normally high in cost. This meant that investments in risk assessment were far higher than risk mitigation. On the contrary, investments in risk mitigation were higher than risk assessment amongst companies in developing economies.

The studies provided an insight into technologies that supported electronic transactions in international banking. Security bottlenecks experienced by end users were also assessed. Human ware was crucial to securing any system. It was found that authentication methods formed the nucleus of any security system. Authentication methods assured customers of key security goals such as confidentiality, integrity and availability. The studies showed that these security goals could be breached if authentication was compromised, unless identification and verification processes within authentication were improved and resolved with appropriate security measures and standards. In the financial sector, the absence of such measures makes information regarding a particular transaction available to attackers and intruders. This could result in a breach of confidentiality which is a key goal of security.

This book presents an overview and critique of online business security systems with emphasis on common electronic commerce activities and payment systems. It discusses legal, compliance and ethical issues that affect management and administration of online business systems. The book introduces the reader to concepts underlying online business systems, as well as technologies that drive online business processes. There is critical evaluation of infrastructure and technologies that support these systems. The role of stakeholders and third parties such as banks, consumers, service providers, traders and regulatory bodies are discussed. Vulnerabilities associated with critical online business infrastructure are highlighted. There is a description of common attacks against online systems and a review of existing security and risk models for securing these systems. Finally this book presents a model and simulation of an integrated approach to security and risk management known as the (SSTM) Service Server Transmission Model for securing Online Business Systems.

Acknowledgements

If writing a book can be a daunting task, the circumstances under which such a piece of work is completed can be even sometimes more challenging. The task can be lighter if the task is shared among family members, friends, and professional colleagues. I received enormous support from such people and institutions. I sincerely thank these people and institutions for their support and kind assistance while putting together this piece of work.

Family

My wife, Sylvia for her untiring help throughout the start and finish of this book

Editorial

- Jhumur Mukherji of East London Business School for editing and proof reading the manuscript and provided advice on the presentation of the book
- Jamil Ampomah of Barclays Bank PLC UK who provided advice on the structure, presentation and editing of the book
- To the unknown reviewers of the manuscript
- Susan and Sharon of Springer-Verlag for their prompt reminders and spot on checks of the formatting of the book

Professional Colleagues and Friends

Raymond, a recent advisor to United Nations Drug and Crime Unit and European Fund security project in Abuja, Nigeria for advising on technical content of the book. Johnness, Chris and Joseph of the innovative research group, University of East London whose expertise and specialty in Malware, Trust and Database security issues served as useful contributions. Isaac K, Principal Engineer and advisor on intelligent systems, Kwasi Karikari USA Patent Office and A, Mellon of SOX Committee for their encouragement.

Appreciation goes to Hesham Kasham my postgraduate Student for collecting data on the Sudan case study that served as a test bed for SSTM (Service Server Transmission Model) security risk analysis.

Affiliations

School of Computing and Technology, University of East London UK

Centre for Research on Computation and Society, Harvard University, USA

Department of Computer Science and Engineering University of Louisville USA

Ghana-India Kofi-Annan Centre of ICT excellence, Ghana

ISACA – Information Systems Control Association, USA, UK

SPIE – International Society of Optical Engineering, USA

AICE Foundation – Advances in Information and Communication Engineering, Foundation, Ghana

Intellas Group, LLC

Chapter 1

Overview of Commercial Activities and Processes in Online Business

1.1   Introduction

This chapter presents an overview of commercial activities and processes that support online business. The chapter examines commercial activities associated with Internet, Cash points, Electronic Point of Sale (EPOS) cash registers, as well as Telephone Banking. There is review of payment systems, gateways as well as intelligent programs known as software agents that facilitate online business activities. The role of stakeholders is also highlighted.

1.2   Commercial Activities and Processes

Zhang and Wang (2003) put into perspective the different categories of commercial activities driven by the Internet. These comprise B2B, B2C and B2G. According to the authors they make up a significant form of e-commerce activities. Even though there is exponential growth in interest with regards to mobile communication, the authors have not mentioned that as a form of commercial activity on its ascendancy. Mobile service applications are deployed for disseminating and transporting information to late night clubbers, workers in the civil service as well as international businessmen in any major city across the world. Mobile communication, B2B, B2C and B2G seem to be the drivers of the new economy, which to a high extent is facilitating the freedom economy. Figures 1 to 4 are conceptual diagrams representing major commercial activities and processes that show sources and destination of personal data in a system. It is designed to enable end users obtain an insight of the internal workings of such systems. Figures 1 to 4 are B2C model activities and processes showing sources and destination of data.

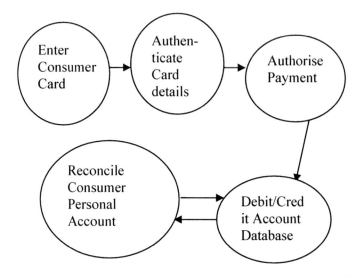

Figure 1 – Internet based activities

1.2.1   Description of Process and Data Flow of Figure 1

In this activity, the consumer enters their debit or credit card details on the web. The details entered are verified for authenticity. The system authorises payment made by the card holder. The card holder's personal bank account or credit card account is debited. There is a reconciliation of consumer's accounts regardless of the payment method. The reconciliation is part of a synchronisation process between a holding account and the consumer's actual account. An electronic data processing specialist will classify this account as a transaction file.

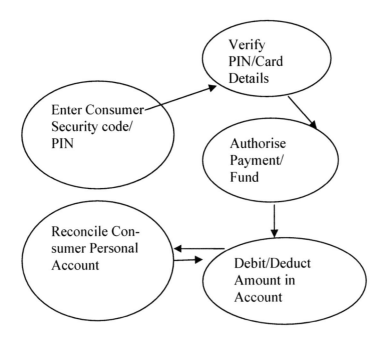

Figure 2 – Automatic Teller Machine (ATM) Process and Data flow diagram

1.2.2   Description of ATM Process and Data Flow in Figure 2

The consumer enters a security code or a personal identification number (PIN) at an Automatic Teller Machine commonly known as a cash point or ATM. The PIN is verified for authenticity. The consumer is prompted to go ahead with any transaction they wish to carryout. At this stage the consumer has direct access to the account. A number of tasks could be completed by the consumer during this period. This could range from electronic fund transfer in the form of a balance transfer to another account, payment of a bill, printing of a statement or checking the balance on an account. These could be considered as the commonest tasks performed by consumers when using ATM. Figure 2 is an illustration of payment of a bill via an ATM. The account of the consumer is debited or deducted. There is a reconciliation of the consumer's personal account. The reconciliation is necessary for a number of reasons. Most banks provide ATM facilities to their customers on different communication networks, regardless of the customer's geographical location. An example is the VISA network. Customers and Consumers whose banks and financial service providers belong to this network could use the facility anywhere. This comes along with a number of distributed communication challenges, such as synchronisation of data and processes across these communication networks. In order to understand this process, carry out this personal experiment. Withdraw funds from any ATM, display or print your balance. Repeat this task at another ATM provider. You are likely to notice that the balances at both ATMs are not the same. This is a synchronisation problem.

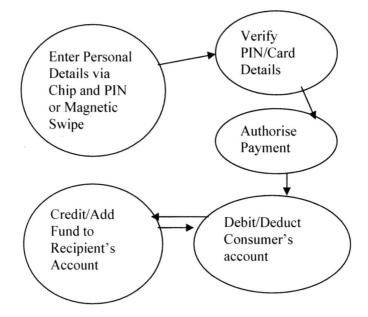

Figure 3 – Electronic Point of Sale (EPOS) Cash Register activities

1.2.3   Description of Process and Data Flow of Figure 3

In an EPOS transaction, the customer or consumer is requested by a customer sales advisor or a smart sales machine to enter card details or swipe a debit or credit card after items selected for purchase have been scanned. The Personal Identification Number (PIN) of the customer is verified. At this stage it is the PIN which is verified for authenticity and not the consumer or customer. Authorisation is then granted to the consumer. The consumer's account is then debited or deducted, followed by a reconciliation of the consumer's account via the service provider's third party's payment system, for example PayPAL.

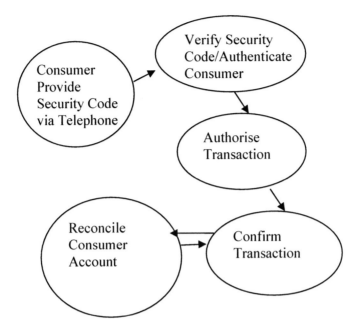

Figure 4 – Telephone banking activities

In this transaction, the consumer provides a security code to a Bank's Customer Service Personnel. The code is verified and authenticated. The transaction requested by the consumer is authorised. The transaction is confirmed while the consumer's account is reconciled. There are a number of security problems associated with telephone banking. The first is the lack of encryption facility on most home telephones. The telephone lines could be eavesdropped. Calls may be diverted to fraudulent providers. The virtual nature of these systems makes them untrustworthy.

1.3   Payments Systems and Gateways

A payment system or gateway is one that is designed to capture funds, authorise the funds and debit or credit a customer's account in real time. Some payment systems are set up to authorise and not debit or credit an account in real time. It is important for the reader to note that payment systems primarily do not authenticate a transaction. They rather authorise them. Examples of payment systems and gateways include, PayPal, 2checkout, CyberSource, HSBC, BT SecPay, DataCash, WireCard, World Pay, eWay, FastCharge, Internet Secure, Secure Hosting etc.

A payment system in general uses an encryption software to secure money which is transferred online. Payment systems do not change how consumers and banks interact. They only serve as mediators or the man in the middle in online transactions. Electronic traders use payment systems as channel for communication and completing online transactions. A fee is usually charged for this online service. Payment systems such as Paypal make money from monies that sit in their accounts during this transaction in the form of an interest. The payment transition between buyers and sellers during online transaction suggest that, there is buffer or holding state of financial details of the buyer and on some occasions the seller. This could serve as an avenue for attack. Customer details such as credit and debit card numbers, bank account numbers and home or personal addresses are vulnerability spots that could be at threat. Some payment systems enable direct transfer of funds from buyer to seller. It is however vital to note that, their operations are based on different models. A key security feature adopted by most payment systems and web services is the "Gausebeck Levchin" test. This technique forces account holders to type in a word found in a small image file on a web page when creating a new account. The technique prevents local or remote execution of scripts which could comprise a text. It is suggested that only humans could read the text on websites if the technique is adopted.

1.3.1   Role of Software Agents in Electronic Payment Systems

This section will describe software agents as contemporary software tools that drive electronic payment systems and Online Business.

1.3.2   What is an Agent?

An agent is anything that can perceive its environment through sensors and act upon that environment through effectors. A human agent has eyes, ears and other sensors that allow it to survive and adapt to its environment (Russel and Norvick 1995). The term performance measure is used to evaluate the criterion used in drawing a conclusion whether an agent is successful or not. Anything that the agent has perceived so far could be called complete perceptual history, the percept sequence. A rational agent is one that does the right thing. The "right" thing might be highly biased in some cases, since what is right in one environment might be wrong in another environment.

The critical success factor is based upon how an agent could perform a particular task. This could be judged on the completeness of the task or other criteria specified by the users or developer. In summary, an agent should be autonomous, adaptive and cooperative in the environment which it operates. These should be inherent parts of the agent. There are different types of agents, these include but not limited to the following; Collaborative agents, link or interface agents, smart agents, internet and mobile agents. These agents function on specific applications and environments. For example mobile agents support mobilization on distributed systems, whiles internet based agents support online business applications such as auctions and billing processing.

http://www.sce.carleton.ca/netmanage/docs/AgentsOverview/ao.html

1.3.3　How does an Agent Behave?

The rational behaviour of an agent is reliant on four factors. These are performance measure, percept sequence, knowledge of environment and actions that the agent could perform. The notion of having an agent able to do the right things such as searching for the right item or product on the Internet might not always be successful. The underpinning rule is that doing what is right might not be necessarily right in another environment. The specification of an agent's activity on the Internet could fail if the agency environment that the agent is operating from, malfunctions.

 A desirable attribute of an agent is that, it should be autonomous. This means that it should not be under the control of another agent, being it software or human. If the agent solely relies on only inherent knowledge, without being able to learn from its environment then it is said that the agent lacks autonomy. Whether an agent lacks autonomy or not, we will need to make a judgment on the implications of using an agent in Online business activities. The next section considers the structure of an agent.

1.3.4　Structure of Agent

The structure of an agent comprises architecture and a program. The architecture is the framework on which the program is built and deployed. The architecture usually comprises percepts, actions, goals and environment. The percept is mapped onto the actions which need to be performed in order to achieve goals in the environment in which it is deployed. Agents usually have the same structure and function, thus accepting percepts and transforming or mapping these percepts to actions in the environment in which they are meant to function. Trust issues related to agents in this section has been examined based on the generic characteristics of an agent without looking into the different types which already exist. This analysis is based on the generic characteristics which cut across most agents.

1.3.5   Agents and Trust in Online Business

The social qualities possessed by software agents due to their adaptive nature on computer networks and distributed system calls for trust. In online business, trust is a critical success factor. A weak trust relationship in any online business is likely to fail. According to Negroponte (1997) an ideal agent has characteristics similar to an English butler who is well trained and knew your needs, likes, habits and desires. The analogy here means that the most trusted agent is the one likely to know your secrets. This assertion could also be verified in the prosecution of Paul Burrell former Butler to Princess Diana, for alleged theft. This is because during Paul Burrell's prosecution, he gave the impression that the Princess confided in him on several occasion. It was also alleged that, he had in his possession personal items belonging to Princess Diana. This leads us to assess trust and its implications on relations in any community, whether human relations or relations among computers.

1.4   What is Trust?

Trust is an intrinsic factor of any living being that influences the extent to which it relies upon information assimilated from known and unknown sources Williams (2004). The key word here is reliability, a characteristic of quality software. Rotter (1980) also defines trust as a general expectancy that the word, oral or written statement of an individual or group of people could be relied upon. Again, the key word here is reliability. Patrick (2002) speculates that when a software agent carries out its instructions then it could be trusted. I think one needs to look beyond that. An agent could serve as a double agent by being loyal to more than one agent. This is seen in the Babington Plot of 1586, when Mary Queen of Scots was imprisoned by Queen Elizabeth the 1st. The encrypted messages from Mary sent to her Catholic supporters via a courier was through a double agent working for Francis Walsingham, Elizabeth's spymaster. Her Cyphertext was broken by Thomas Phelipes, master forger and cryptanalyst for Sir Francis Harrison (2004). Applying trust in software agents for Online Business activities suggest that control functions are made void, when the software agent is allowed to determine its own existence. What controls do developers put in place in order to achieve such a level of reliability? For example, is there a rule or policy that enforces loyalty within only one agency? Or does an agency have a rule or policy that verifies signs of disloyalty? These are example of checks and balances that could be put in place. The issue of trust is highly dependent on the checks and balances implemented as part of the software agent commissioned to perform Online search and auction activities. Zan (1972) asserts that we need trust because we are vulnerable. However, that is not always the case. Although that might be the case in certain circumstances, trust might be needed in circumstances where relationships amongst people need to thrive or progress in order to achieve greater goals. Remember the performance measure, the criteria used in determining success in software agents. The next section examines conditions likely to influence trust.

1.4.1   Conditions Likely to Affect Trust

Given the definitions and examples of trust situations, it could be argued that trust is relative and subjective. It should be assessed and judged in a given context. The survey of Cranor, Reagle and Akerman (2000) suggest that different people have different threshold for trust. This means that the criterion and balances put in place to manage the behaviour of a software agent might not be applicable to every circumstance.

Patrick (2002) highlights six (6) factors discussed in conjunction with Lee, Kim and Moon's model of agent success. These factors are ability to trust, experience, predictable performance, comprehensive information, communication and interface design, presentation and certification and logos of assurance. Their findings were drawn from a survey conducted on Internet users. These conditions are likely to change from one circumstance to another. These conditions could also be influenced by society and environment.

Wong and Sycara (1999) propose a framework for addressing security and trust issues that could be assessed and tested in Online Business environments. According to the authors, adding security and trust improve users' confidence and assurance when a task is assigned to them. They indicate a number of factors that influence the level of confidence necessary to trust a system. These include corrupted naming and matchmaking services, insecure communication channels, insecure delegation and lack of accountability. Although each factor mentioned is important, insecure communication channels and insecure delegation are highly sensitive risk factors which if not managed effectively will degrade the level of trust and confidence that a user places on an Online System. This is due to the fact that communication networks that support distributed platforms exhibit risk access spots (RAS) which make them susceptible to attacks Williams (2003). These in secure communication channels include ports, random access memory (RAM), poor configuration of firewalls, communication media both wired and wireless networks and router tables Williams (2003). With regards to insecure delegation there are issues related to authenticity of the agent. Is the agent what it claims to be? How do we verify this level of authenticity? Are there any methods based on empirical evidence? Or do we apply a general security model? These are questions that have not been answered satisfactorily.

Das (2003) examines payment agents by presenting a model of software agents. These agents serve as tools for making payments on behalf of clients. The model is satisfactorily articulated by highlighting both application areas and threats associated with their application on communication networks. Mobile applications with intelligent capabilities and functions drive critical electronic commerce activities. There are different agents that facilitate transactions through mobility from one computer network to another. The main phases of a secured payment protocol for agents are; withdrawal, distribution, payment, verification and transfer phases.

Digital cash schemes could be classified into digital cash, fair digital and Brand's digital cash. These consist of four phases, thus opening an account, withdrawal, payment and deposit. Mu, Varadharajan and Nguyen (2003) explore concerns likely to be raised by law enforcement agencies. They believe that it might serve as a haven for criminal activities due to the nature of the system and policies that accompany the processing of transactions. This makes large scale deployment a nightmare. Clear notational representation of concepts for the setup, the process of opening an account, the withdrawal process, payment process and the deposit process should be understood by the payment agent. It is appropriate for developers who want to explore the different digital schemes, design concepts and associated protocols in conjunction with payment agents, to understand the stages involved in such transaction.

1.4.2   Micro Payment Systems

A micro payment system is a system that supports transactions involving very small amounts of money. The amount could range from 0.100 cents, 0.100 pence or 0.10 pesewa. The system could be used for credit point accumulation on club cards and credit cards. It can also be used for payments and charges associated with transport systems.

Herzberg (2003) discusses the practicalities and challenges related to micro payment systems. The assessment provides a conceptual view and likewise discusses issues that have to be addressed in order for micro payments systems to function effectively. PSP (Payment Service Providers) provide a charging scheme which is acceptable to clients and merchants alike. There is an overview of micro payment visa PSP model. It is suggested in this book that a presentation and discussion on a range of models would have been useful in illustrating the different transaction models between merchant, customer and PSP that existed. The major categories of cost are also discussed. The information will be highly essential to practitioners who intend to develop or conduct investigations on models critical in assessing cost of disputes, charge backs, customer support, equipment, processing and communication cost, bookkeeping, auditing, point of sale and credit risk. There is detail explanation of charges associated with disputes. It provides a general and broad understanding for researchers who aim to gain knowledge with regards to the rules and legalities that protect the interest of consumers, obligations of merchants as well as service providers. There are also discussions of servers that support such systems. For distributed systems engineers, this is something to explore.

1.5   Role of Stakeholders in Online Business

- **Consumer**

The Consumer is central and pivotal to all commercial activities, as such the most important element within the supply chain of products and services. This means that providing the most effective security system and efficient services for delivery become paramount and top of the agenda for service providers. Consumer technologies such as telephones, mobile and smart phones, mobile computers with Satellite, Infra-Red, Bluetooth, Wireless Local Area Network capabilities are all information communication technologies used by consumers to engage in electronic commerce and online business activities. Figure 5 is an example of recent security improvements announced by Lloyds TSB to improve security for their customers. This is designed to alleviate the fears of their customers.

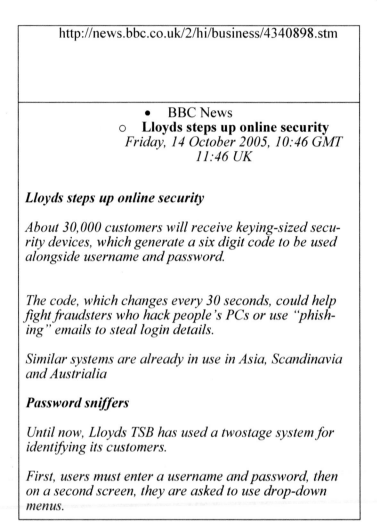

Figure 5 – BBC webpage showing new online security measure introduced by Lloyds TSB to protect Consumers

- **Banks**

Banks are institutions that provide financial services. Today, most Banks have innovated from brick walls to online banking. In general online banking connotes banking via the Internet. However it has a broader meaning than banking via Internet. Online Banking can also involve technologies such as telephone, Automatic Tele Machines (ATM) and mobile phones. Nowadays, ATMs can provide most basic financial services except perhaps application for a loan.

- **Service Providers**

Service Providers could be classified into two main groups. The first is technology providers, and the second is institutions that provide auxiliary financial services. Examples of the foremost are British Telecom (BT), American Online (AOL), GOOGLE, E-bay, √eriSign etc. Auxiliary financial services include VISA and Capital One. whiles the latter include credit unions, financial advisory agencies and payment system providers.

- **Traders**

Traders are described as individuals, institutions or bodies that sell products or services with the sole aim of making profit. Whiles companies have broader objectives, such as achieving high productivity as well as profitability, Traders and Sellers focus strongly on making profit. Productivity is not a critical success factor. Online Business has provided unlimited opportunity to people to partake in what is termed in this book as "pseudo trading" a term coined to signify non traditional methods of trading by third parties through the Internet. Example of "pseudo trading" is selling a book through Amazon, GOOGLE or a car via EBay. There are security and trust issues associated with such purchase. This includes absence of a business model that integrates such a trade. There are also concerns regarding the virtual nature of the entire transaction.

- **Regulatory Bodies**

Regulatory bodies usually enforce or serve as referees in business by enforcing fair trade. They also moderate the operations of businesses and traders. They serve as a watchdog and protect the interest of the consumer, although the latter is not always the case. They also ensure adherence to appropriate business ethics. These organisations include professional societies and Government agencies such as the Department of Trade and Industry, Organisation for Fair Trade in UK, Department for Trade and Commerce, British Standard Institute (BSI) and Law Societies. The World Trade Organisation (WTO) of the United Nations, which seem to have come under criticism in recent times from developing economies, for not enforcing global fair trade, the National Institute of Standards and Technology (NIST) of the United States of America and Bank for International Settlements in ASIA, which fosters international monetary and financial cooperation and serves as a bank for central banks.

1.6   Summary

Chapter 1 provided an overview of commercial activities and processes in Online Business. The chapter gave an insight of activities associated with Internet based activities, Automatic Teller Machines or Cash points, Electronic Point of Sale (EPOS) cash register activities and Telephone Banking. There was also an introduction to payment systems and Gateways and how they worked. Examples of payment systems included PayPal, FastCharge and CyberSource. The processes common to all these commercial activities included authentication, authorisation and answerability. There was introduction to Software agents as vehicles and facilitators of payment systems. The chapter also evaluated role of micro payment systems in a broader context. The role of stakeholders was reviewed. There was mention of stakeholders such as consumers, banks, service providers, traders, sellers and regulatory bodies.

Chapter 2

Legal and Socio-Ethical Issues in Online Business

2.1   Introduction

This chapter reviews and discusses legal and socio-ethical requirements that affect Online Business activities. There is particular reference to Internet law with respect to interpretations of different aspects of the Law. Some of the laws covered in the chapter includes, Fraud and Abuse Act of 1986, Computer Misuse Act of 1990, Copyright, Electronic Communication Privacy Act 2000 and the data protection Act of UK 2000. Email and Privacy Laws usually covering email policy, email privacy, monitoring employees, Right of Privacy in Online applications, Crypto-systems, Online Games and Gambling, and most importantly the Telephone consumer Act of 1991.

2.2   Legislation and Law

The global reach of the Internet makes it an ideal tool for international business beyond traditional business channels in an information society. The rapid deployment of commercial web sites globally shows the importance of this cost-effective possibility for businesses to present themselves in a global market place, Bernard Glasson et al (30, 31, 34). In view of this new marketing and business age, using sophisticated technology in Online business activities have become more complex than the years before. The law regulating the behaviour of individuals and businesses with the advent of advance technology in this regard is not as effective as one will expect it to be, within the broader context of international law.

In his article "net can't catch cyber criminals" Rob Jones expressed the worries and frustrations of Albert Pacey the director general of the national criminal intelligence service (NCIS) UK. The boss of the intelligence service warned that it was needed to criminalise the theft of electronic data. He was speaking to delegates from police forces around the world, at the organised crime conference in London to discuss how they combat the (IT) criminal class. To summarise his words, he said "change the law or face the growth of a new criminal class" Jones R (1997).

In retrospect the NCIS boss's proposition was arguably valid in the sense that looking into the embedded issues of security for funds transfer and information in general, the possible solutions lies in the hands of Governments rather than information technologists. It is Governments because, the issue is international not national. Any approach used by a particular nation's Government to resolve this issue which reflects a national approach is more likely to fail. In view of this, there is the need to adopt a strategy that takes into consideration specific countries legal framework and culture. This is because we are in a global economic information age, as such all issues surrounding security of Online Business should be addressed globally. It will therefore be just an illusion of success if a global approach is not adopted.

Although the electronic communications privacy act of 1986 specifically forbids eaves dropping on electronic transmissions, laws of that kind are extra-ordinarily difficult to enforce, because no policing agency controls the points of access Spar D and Jeffery J (1996). Since the core cause of this problem is international rather than national, it will be very much appropriate for us to examine the impact of international law on this issue.

2.2.1   International Law

The simplest definition of international law believed ever defined is "a system of rules governing the relations between sovereign states". Let us take a particular interest in the word sovereign or sovereignty Dixon M (306, 138, 276). According to the oxford dictionary, it means supremacy, self Government or a self Governing State. It is important for us to note that for the sovereignty of a state to be recognised in the purview of law, its jurisdiction must be clearly defined.

Jurisdiction is the extent of a nation's legal or territorial authority. In other words where it can administer justice, play a crucial role in the contribution to information security management of Online Business. This is because globalisation of information transfer cuts across the boundaries of nations.

2.2.1.1 Limitations of International Law

It is the limitation of international law in this regard why concerned people like Albert Pacey, and other passionate members of the information research community fear that current state of cyber-crime if not managed effectively will get out of hand. Although some part of the law empowers nations to arrest and prosecute individuals who might commit a crime against any of its institutions. It only works where the criminal's nation or where s/he takes refuge corporate in the arrest and prosecution. It must be noted that this aspect of the law mostly applies exclusively outside the scope of information technology, due to the fact that laws covering computer crime needs further development and enforcement globally. In order for us to get a better picture concerning this aspect of the law, let us examine the Harvard research convention on jurisdiction with respect to crime (1935). "A state has jurisdiction with respect to any crime committed outside it's territory by an alien against the security, territorial integrity or political independence of that state, provided that the act or omission which constitutes the crime was not committed in exercise of a liberty guaranteed the alien by law of the place where it was committed".

Social order and the coexistence of states make it important for boundaries between their sovereignties and jurisdictions. This is because contradiction of every state's power is inevitably involved. The American law institute defines jurisdiction as "the capacity of a state under international law to prescribe or enforce a rule of law". The institute's definition draws attention to the distinction between a state's jurisdiction to prescribe and to enforce law. A state can not enforce a law it has no right to prescribe. However a state may prescribe a law it may be unable to enforce. For instance if a criminal commits a crime and escapes into another states jurisdiction, and that state has no good international relations with state that the crime was committed against, the affected state has no right to extend it's judicial powers in that state Levi W (107).

Poor international relations grossly contribute to the ineffectiveness of the law. It is a real unforeseen menace that lies ahead of Online Business global community.

There are independent organisations that provide advice to consumers with respect to these Acts. These organisations include; The Online Privacy Alliance, (AUCE) European coalition for unsolicited emails, Crypto Law Society and Australian Privacy Foundation. Section 1.6 presents the Electronic Communication Privacy Act as applied in the USA. This is designed to provide relevant information regarding the legal implications in case of violation or an incident of abuse with respect to privacy in places where similar Acts of Law exist. You may skip this section if you are already familiar with this particular Act.

2.2.2   Internet Law

Section 2.1.1 presents a compilation from Phillips Nizer LLP (2007) on
Electronic Communication Privacy Act 47 U.S.C Section 230, Electronic
Communications Privacy Act, Stored Wire and Electronic Communications
and Transactional Records Access.

18 U.S.C. §§ 2701-2711

§ 2701. Unlawful Access to Stored Communications

(a) Offence - Except as provided in subsection (c) of this section whoever -

(1) intentionally accesses without authorization a facility through which an
electronic communication service is provided; or

(2) intentionally exceeds an authorization to access that facility; and
thereby obtains, alters, or prevents authorized access to a wire or electronic
communication while it is in electronic storage in such system shall be pun-
ished as provided in subsection (b) of this section.

(b) Punishment - The punishment for an offence under subsection (a) of
this subsection is -

(1) if the offence is committed for purposes of commercial advantage,
malicious destruction or damage, or private commercial gain -

(A) a fine under this title or imprisonment for not more than one year, or
both, in the case of a first offence under this subparagraph; and

(B) a fine under this title or imprisonment for not more than two years, or
both, for any subsequent offence under this subparagraph; and

(2) a fine under this title or imprisonment for not more than six months, or
both, in any other case.

(c) Exceptions - Subsection (a) of this section does not apply with respect
to conduct authorized

(1) by the person or entity providing a wire or electronic communications
service;

(2) by a user of that service with respect to a communication of or intended
for that user; or

(3) in section 2703, 2704 or 2518 of this title.

§ 2702. Disclosure of Contents

(a) Prohibitions - Except as provided in subsection (b) -

(1) a person or entity providing an electronic communication service to the public shall not knowingly divulge to any person or entity the contents of a communication while in electronic storage by that service; and

(2) a person or entity providing remote computing service to the public shall not knowingly divulge to any person or entity the contents of any communication which is carried or maintained on that service -

(A) on behalf of, and received by means of electronic transmission from (or created by means of computer processing of communications received by means of electronic transmission from), a subscriber or customer of such service; and

(B) Solely for the purpose of providing storage or computer processing services to such subscriber or customer, if the provider is not authorized to access the contents of any such communications for purposes of providing any services other than storage or computer processing.

(b) Exceptions - A person or entity may divulge the contents of a communication

(1) to an addressee or intended recipient of such communication or an agent of such addressee or intended recipient

(2) as otherwise authorized in section 2517, 2511(2)(a), or 2703 of this title;

(3) with the lawful consent of the originator or an addressee or intended recipient of such communication, or the subscriber in the case of remote computing service;

(4) to a person employed or authorized or whose facilities are used to forward such communication to its destination;

(5) as may be necessarily incident to the rendition of the service or to the protection of the rights or property of the provider of that service; or

(6) to a law enforcement agency -

(A) if such contents -

(i) were inadvertently obtained by the service provider; and

(ii) appear to pertain to the commission of a crime.

(B) if required by section 227 of the Crime Control Act of 1990.

§ 2703. Requirements for Governmental Access

(a) Contents of Electronic Communications in Electronic Storage - A governmental entity may require the disclosure by a provider of electronic communication service of the contents of an electronic communication, that is in electronic storage in an electronic communications system for one hundred and eighty days or less, only pursuant to a warrant issued under the Federal Rules of Criminal Procedure or equivalent State warrant. A governmental entity may require the disclosure by a provider of electronic communications services of the contents of an electronic communication that has been in electronic storage in an electronic communications system for more than one hundred and eighty days by the means available under subsection (b) of this section.

(b) Contents of Electronic Communications in a Remote Computing Service -

(1) A governmental entity may require a provider of remote computing service to disclose the contents of any electronic communication to which this paragraph is made applicable by paragraph (2) of this subsection -

(A) without required notice to the subscriber or customer, if the governmental entity obtains a warrant issued under the Federal Rules of Criminal Procedure or equivalent State warrant; or

(B) with prior notice from the governmental entity to the subscriber or customer if the governmental entity -

(i) uses an administrative subpoena authorized by a Federal or State statute or a Federal or State grand jury or trial subpoena; or

(ii) obtains a court order for such disclosure under subsection (d) of this section; except that delayed notice may be given pursuant to section 2705 of this title.

(2) Paragraph (1) is applicable with respect to any electronic communication that is held or maintained on that service -

(A) on behalf of, and received by means of electronic transmission from (or created by means of computer processing of communications received by means of electronic transmission from), a subscriber or customer of such remote computing service; and

(B) solely for the purpose of providing storage or computer processing services to such subscriber or customer, if the provider is not authorized to access the contents of any such communications for purpose of providing any services other than storage or computer processing.

(c) Records Concerning Electronic Communication Service or Remote Computing Service -

(1)(A) Except as provided in subparagraph (B), a provider of electronic communication service or remote computing service may disclose a record or other information pertaining to a subscriber to or customer of such service (not including the contents of communications covered by subsection (a) or (b) of this section) to any person other than a governmental entity.

(B) A provider of electronic communication service or remote computing service shall disclose a record or other information pertaining to a subscriber to or customer of such service (not including the contents of communications covered by subsection (a) or (b) of this section) to a governmental entity only when the governmental entity -

(i) obtains a warrant issued under the Federal Rules of Criminal Procedure or equivalent State warrant;

(ii) obtains a court order for such disclosure under subsection (d) of this section;

(iii) has the consent of the subscriber or customer to such disclosure; or

(iv) submits a formal written request relevant to a law enforcement investigation concerning telemarketing fraud for the name, address, and place of business of a subscriber or customer of such provider, which subscriber or customer is engaged in telemarketing (as such term is defined in section 2325 of this title).

(C) A provider of electronic communication service or remote computing service shall disclose to a governmental entity the name, address, local and long distance telephone toll billing records, telephone number or other subscriber number or identity, and length of service of a subscriber to or customer of such service and the types of services the subscriber or customer utilized, when the governmental entity uses an administrative subpoena authorized by a Federal or State statute or a Federal or State grand jury or trial subpoena or any means available under subparagraph (B).

(2) A governmental entity receiving records or information under this subsection is not required to provide notice to a subscriber or customer.

(d) Requirements for Court Order - A court order for disclosure under subsection (b) or (c) may be issued by any court that is a court of competent jurisdiction described in section 3127(2)(A) and shall issue only if the governmental entity offers specific facts showing that there are reasonable grounds to believe that the contents of a wire or electronic communication, or the records or other information sought, are relevant and material to an ongoing criminal investigation. In the case of a State governmental authority, such a court order shall not issue if prohibited by the law of such State. A court issuing an order pursuant to this section, on a motion made promptly by the service provider, may quash or modify such order, if the information or records requested are unusually voluminous in nature or compliance with such order otherwise would cause an undue burden on such provider.

(e) No Cause of Action Against a Provider Disclosing Information Under This Chapter - No cause of action shall lie in any court against any provider of wire or electronic communication service, its officers, employees, agents, or other specified persons for providing information, facilities, or assistance in accordance with the terms of a court order, warrant, subpoena, or certification under this chapter.

(f) Requirement to Preserve Evidence -

(1) In general - A provider of wire or electronic communication services or a remote computing service, upon the request of a governmental entity, shall take all necessary steps to preserve records and other evidence in its possession pending the issuance of a court order or other process.

(2) Period of retention - Records referred to in paragraph (1) shall be retained for a period of 90 days, which shall be extended for an additional 90 day period upon a renewed request by the governmental entity. §2704. Backup Preservation.

(a) Backup Preservation -

(1) A governmental entity acting under section 2703(b)(2) may include in its subpoena or court order a requirement that the service provider to whom the request is directed create a backup copy of the contents of the electronic communications sought in order to preserve those communications. Without notifying the subscriber or customer of such subpoena or court order, such service provider shall create such backup copy as soon as practicable consistent with its regular business practices and shall confirm to the governmental entity that such backup copy has been made. Such backup copy shall be created within two business days after receipt by the service provider of the subpoena or court order.

(2) Notice to the subscriber or customer shall be made by the governmental entity within three days after receipt of such confirmation, unless such notice is delayed pursuant to section 2705(a).

(3) The service provider shall not destroy such backup copy until the later of (A) the delivery of the information; or

(B) the resolution of any proceedings (including appeals of any proceeding) concerning the government's subpoena or court order

(4) The service provider shall release such backup copy to the requesting governmental entity no sooner than fourteen days after the governmental entity's notice to the subscriber or customer if such service provider -

(A) has not received notice from the subscriber or customer that the subscriber or customer has challenged the governmental entity's request; and

(B) has not initiated proceedings to challenge the request of the governmental entity. (5) A governmental entity may seek to require the creation of a backup copy under subsection (a)(1) of this section if in its sole discretion such entity determines that there is reason to believe that notification under section 2703 of this title of the existence of the subpoena or court order may result in destruction of or tampering with evidence. This determination is not subject to challenge by the subscriber or customer or service provider.

(b) Customer Challenges -

(1) Within fourteen days after notice by the governmental entity to the subscriber or customer under subsection (a)(2) of this section, such subscriber

or customer may file a motion to quash such subpoena or vacate such court order, with copies served upon the governmental entity and with written notice of such challenge to the service provider. A motion to vacate a court order shall be filed in the court which issued such order. A motion to quash a subpoena shall be filed in the appropriate United States district court or State court. Such motion or application shall contain an affidavit or sworn statement -

(A) stating that the application is a customer or subscriber to the service from which the contents of electronic communications maintained for him have been sought; and

(B) Stating the applicant's reasons for believing that the records sought are not relevant to a legitimate law enforcement inquiry or that there has not been substantial compliance with the provisions of this chapter in some other respect.

(2) Service shall be made under this section upon a governmental entity by delivering or mailing by registered or certified mail a copy of the papers to the person, office, or department specified in the notice which the customer has received pursuant to this chapter. For the purposes of this section, the term "delivery" has the meaning given that term in the Federal Rules of Civil Procedure.

(3) If the court finds that the customer has complied with paragraphs (1) and (2) of this subsection, the court shall order the governmental entity to file a sworn response, which may be filed in camera if the governmental entity includes in its response the reasons which make in camera review appropriate. If the court is unable to determine the motion or application on the basis of the parties' initial allegations and response, the court may conduct such additional proceedings as it deems appropriate. All such proceedings shall be completed and the motion or application decided as soon as practicable after the filing of the governmental entity's response.

(4) If the court finds that the applicant is not the subscriber or customer for whom the communications sought by the governmental entity are maintained, or that there is a reason to believe that the law enforcement inquiry is legitimate and that the communications sought are relevant to that inquiry, it shall deny the motion or application and order such process enforced. If the court finds that the applicant is the subscriber or customer for whom the communications sought by the governmental entity are maintained, and that there is not a reason to believe that the communications

sought are relevant to a legitimate law enforcement inquiry, or that there has not been substantial compliance with the provisions of this chapter, it shall order the process quashed.

(5) A court order denying a motion or application under this section shall not be deemed a final order and no interlocutory appeal may be taken there from by the customer. §2705. Delayed Notice

(a) Delay of Notification -

(1) A governmental entity acting under section 2703(b) of this title may -

(A) where a court order is sought, include in the application a request, which the court shall grant, for an order delaying the notification required under section 2703(b) of this title for a period not to exceed ninety days, if the court determines that there is reason to believe that notification of the existence of the court order may have an adverse result described in paragraph (2) of this subsection; or

(B) where an administrative subpoena authorized by a Federal or State statute or a Federal or State grand jury subpoena is obtained, delay the notification required under section 2703(b) of this title for a period not to exceed ninety days upon the execution of a written certification of a supervisory official that there is reason to believe that notification of the existence of the subpoena may have an adverse result described in paragraph (2) of this subsection.

(2) An adverse result for the purposes of paragraph (1) of this subsection is -

(A) endangering the life or physical safety of an individual;

(B) flight from prosecution;

(C) destruction of or tampering with evidence;

(D) intimidation of potential witnesses; or

(E) otherwise seriously jeopardizing an investigation or unduly delaying a trial.

(3) The governmental entity shall maintain a true copy of certification under paragraph (1)(B).

(4) Extensions of the delay of notification provided in section 2703 of up to ninety days each may be granted by the court upon application or by certification by a governmental entity, but only in accordance with subsection (b) of this section.

(5) Upon expiration of the period of delay of notification under paragraph (1) or (4) of this subsection, the governmental entity shall serve upon, or deliver by registered or first-class mail to, the customer or subscriber a copy of the process or request together with notice that -

(A) states with reasonable specificity the nature of the law enforcement inquiry; and

(B) informs such customer or subscriber -

(i) that information maintained for such customer or subscriber by the service provider named in such process or request was supplied to or requested by that governmental authority and the date on which the supplying or request took place;

(ii) that notification of such customer or subscriber was delayed;

(iii) what governmental entity or court made the certification or determination pursuant to which that delay was made; and

(iv) which provision of this chapter allowed such delay.

(6) As used in this subsection, the term "supervisory official" means the investigative agent in charge or assistant investigative agent in charge or an equivalent of an investigating agency's headquarters or regional office, or the chief prosecuting attorney or the first assistant prosecuting attorney or an equivalent of a prosecuting attorney's headquarters or regional office.

(b) Preclusion of Notice to Subject of Governmental Access - A governmental entity acting under section 2703, when it is not required to notify the subscriber or customer under section 2703(b)(1), or to the extent that it may delay such notice pursuant to subsection (a) of this section, may apply to a court for an order commanding a provider of electronic communications service or remote computing service to whom a warrant, subpoena, or court order is directed, for such period as the court deems appropriate, not to notify any other person of the existence of the warrant, subpoena, or court order. The court shall enter such an order if it determines that there is reason to believe that notification of the existence of the warrant, subpoena, or court order will result in -

(1) endangering the life or physical safety of an individual;

(2) flight from prosecution;

(3) destruction of or tampering with evidence;

(4) intimidation of potential witnesses; or

(5) Otherwise seriously jeopardizing an investigation or unduly delaying a trial.

§2706. Cost Reimbursement

(a) Payment - Except as otherwise provided in subsection (c), a governmental entity obtaining the contents of communications, records, or other information under section 2702, 2703, or 2704 of this title shall pay to the person or entity assembling or providing such information a fee for reimbursement for such costs as are reasonably necessary and which have been directly incurred in searching for, assembling, reproducing, or otherwise providing such information. Such reimbursable costs shall include any costs due to necessary disruption of normal operations of any electronic communication service or remote computing service in which such information may be stored.

(b) Amount - The amount of the fee provided by subsection (a) shall be as mutually agreed by the governmental entity and the person or entity providing the information, or, in the absence of agreement, shall be determined by the court which issued the order for production of such information (or the court before which a criminal prosecution relating to such information would be brought, if no court order was issued for production of the information).

(c) Exception - The requirement of subsection (a) of this section does not apply with respect to records or other information maintained by a communications common carrier that relate to telephone toll records and telephone listings obtained under section 2703 of this title. The court may, however, order a payment as described in subsection (a) if the court determines the information required is unusually voluminous in nature or otherwise caused an undue burden on the provider.

§ 2707. Civil Action

(a) Cause of Action - Except as provided in section 2703(e), any provider of electronic communication service, subscriber, or customer aggrieved by any violation of this chapter in which the conduct constituting the violation is engaged in with a knowing or intentional state of mind may, in a civil action, recover from the person or entity which engaged in that violation such relief as may be appropriate.

(b) Relief - In a civil action under this section, appropriate relief includes -

(1) such preliminary and other equitable or declaratory relief as may be appropriate;

(2) damages under subsection (c); and

(3) a reasonable attorney's fee and other litigation costs reasonably incurred.

(c) Damages - The court may assess as damages in a civil action under this section the sum of the actual damages suffered by the plaintiff and any profits made by the violator as a result of the violation, but in no case shall a person entitled to recover receive less than the sum of $1,000. If the violation is willful or intentional, the court may assess punitive damages. In the case of a successful action to enforce liability under this section, the court may assess the costs of the action, together with reasonable attorney fees determined by the court.

(d) Disciplinary Actions for Violations - If a court determines that any agency or department of the United States has violated this chapter and the court finds that the circumstances surrounding the violation raise the question whether or not an officer or employee of the agency or department acted willfully or intentionally with respect to the violation, the agency or department concerned shall promptly initiate a proceeding to determine whether or not disciplinary action is warranted against the officer or employee.

(e) Defence - A good faith reliance on -

(1) a court warrant or order, a grand jury subpoena, a legislative authorization, or a statutory authorization;

(2) a request of an investigative or law enforcement officer under section 2518(7) of this title; or

(3) a good faith determination that section 2511(3) of this title permitted the conduct complained of;

is a complete defence to any civil or criminal action brought under this chapter or any other law.

(f) Limitation - A civil action under this section may not be commenced later than two years after the date upon which the claimant first discovered or had a reasonable opportunity to discover the violation.

§ 2708. Exclusivity of Remedies

The remedies and sanctions described in this chapter are the only judicial remedies and sanctions for no constitutional violations of this chapter.

§2709. Counterintelligence Access to Telephone Toll and Transactional Records

(a) Duty to Provide - A wire or electronic communication service provider shall comply with a request for subscriber information and toll billing records information, or electronic communication transactional records in its custody or possession made by the Director of the Federal Bureau of Investigation under subsection (b) of this section.

(b) Required Certification - The Director of the Federal Bureau of Investigation, or his designee in a position not lower than Deputy Assistant Director, may -

(1) request the name, address, length of service, and local and long distance toll billing records of a person or entity if the Director (or his designee in a position not lower than Deputy Assistant Director) certifies in writing to the wire or electronic communication service provider to which the request is made that -

(A) the name address, length of service, and toll billing records sought are relevant to an authorized foreign counterintelligence investigation; and

(B) there are specific facts giving reason to believe that the person or entity to whom the information sought pertains is a foreign power or an agent of a foreign power as defined in section 101 of the Foreign Intelligence Surveillance Act of 1978 (50 U.S.C. 1801); and

(2) request the name, address, and length of service of a person or entity if the Director (or his designee in a position not lower than Deputy Assistant Director) certifies in writing to the wire or electronic communication service provider to which the request is made that -

(A) the information sought is relevant to an authorized foreign counterintelligence investigation; and

(B) there are specific facts giving reason to believe that communication facilities registered in the name of the person or entity have been used, through the services of such provider, in communication with -

(i) an individual who is engaging or has engaged international terrorism as defined in section 101(c) of the Foreign Intelligence Surveillance Act or clandestine intelligence activities that involve or may involve a violation of the criminal statutes of the United States; or

(ii) a foreign power or an agent of a foreign power under circumstances giving reason to believe that the communication concerned international terrorism as defined in section 101(c) of the Foreign Intelligence Surveillance Act or clandestine intelligence activities that involve or may involve a violation of the criminal statutes of the United States.

(c) Prohibition of Certain Disclosure - No wire or electronic communication service provider, or officer, employee, or agent thereof, shall disclose to any person that the Federal Bureau of Investigation has sought or obtained access to information or records under this section.

(d) Dissemination by Bureau - The Federal Bureau of Investigation may disseminate information and records obtained under this section only as provided in guidelines approved by the Attorney General for foreign intelligence collection and foreign counterintelligence investigations conducted by the Federal Bureau of Investigation, and, with respect to dissemination to an agency of the United States, only if such information is clearly relevant to the authorized responsibilities of such agency.

(e) Requirement That Certain Congressional Bodies Be Informed - On a semiannual basis the Director of the Federal Bureau of Investigation shall fully inform the Permanent Select Committee on Intelligence of the House of Representatives and the Select Committee on Intelligence of the Senate, and the Committee on the Judiciary of the House of Representatives and the Committee on the Judiciary of the Senate, concerning all requests made under subsection (b) of this section.

§ 2710. Wrongful Disclosure of Video Tape Rental or Sale Records

(a) Definitions - For purposes of this section -

(1) the term "consumer" means any renter, purchaser, or subscriber of goods or services from a video tape service provider;

(2) the term "ordinary course of business" means only debt collection activities, order fulfilment, request processing, and the transfer of ownership;

(3) the term "personally identifiable information" includes information which identifies a person as having requested or obtained specific video materials or services from a video tape service provider; and

(4) the term "video tape service provider" means any person, engaged in the business, in or affecting interstate or foreign commerce, of rental, sale, or delivery of pre-recorded video cassette tapes or similar audio visual materials, or any person or other entity to whom a disclosure is made under subparagraph (D) or (E) of subsection (b)(2), but only with respect to the information contained in the disclosure.

(b) Video Tape Rental and Sale Records -

(1) A video tape service provider who knowingly discloses, to any person, personally identifiable information concerning any consumer of such provider shall be liable to the aggrieved person for the relief provided in subsection (d);

(2) A video tape service provided may disclose personally identifiable information concerning any consumer -

(A) to the consumer;

(B) to any person with the informed, written consent of the consumer given at the time the disclosure is sought;

(C) to a law enforcement agency pursuant to a warrant issued under the Federal Rules of Criminal Procedure, an equivalent State warrant, a grand jury subpoena, or a court order;

(D) to any person if the disclosure is solely of the names and addresses of consumers and if -

(i) the video tape service provider had provided the consumer with the opportunity, in a clear and conspicuous manner, to prohibit such disclosure; and

(ii) the disclosure does not identify the title, description, or subject matter of any video tapes or other audio visual material; however, the subject matter of such materials may be disclosed if the disclosure is for the exclusive use of marketing goods and services directly to the consumer;

(E) to any person if the disclosure is incident to the ordinary course of business of the video taper service provider; or

(F) pursuant to a court order, in a civil proceeding upon a showing of compelling need for the information that cannot be accommodated by any other means, if -

(i) the consumer is given reasonable notice, by the person seeking the disclosure of the court proceeding relevant to the issuance of the court order; and

(ii) the consumer is afforded the opportunity to appear and contest the claim of the person seeking the disclosure. If an order is granted pursuant to subparagraph (C) or (F), the court shall impose appropriate safeguards against unauthorized disclosure.

(3) Court orders authorizing disclosure under subparagraph (C) shall issue only with prior notice to the consumer and only if the law enforcement agency shows that there is probable cause to believe that the records or other information sought are relevant to a legitimate law enforcement inquiry. In the case of a State government authority, such a court order shall not issue if prohibited by the law of such State. A court issuing an order pursuant to this section, on a motion made promptly by the video tape service provider, may quash or modify such order if the information or records requested are unreasonably voluminous in nature or if compliance with such order otherwise would cause an unreasonable burden on such provider.

(c) Civil Action -

(d) Any person aggrieved by any act of a person in violation of this section may bring a civil action in a United States district court (e)(2) The court may award -

(A) actual damage but not less than liquidated damages in an amount of $2,500;

(B) punitive damages;

(C) reasonable attorneys' fees and other litigation costs reasonably incurred; and

(D) such other preliminary and equitable relief as the court determines to be appropriate.

(3) No action may be brought under this subsection unless such action is begun within 2 years from the date of the act complained of or the date of discovery.

(4) No liability shall result from lawful disclosure permitted by this section.

(f) Personally Identifiable Information - Personally identifiable information obtained in any manner other than as provided in this section shall not be received in evidence in any trial, hearing, arbitration, or other proceeding in or before any court, grand jury, department, officer, agency, regulatory body, legislative committee, or other authority of the United States, a State or a political subdivision of a State.

(g) Destruction of Old Records - A person subject to this section shall destroy personally identifiable information as soon as practicable, but no later than one year from the date the information is no longer necessary for the purpose for which it was collected and there are no pending requests or orders for access to such information under subsection (b)(2) or (c)(2) or pursuant to a court order.

(h) Preemption - The provisions of this section preempt only the provisions of State or local law that require disclosure prohibited by this section.

§ 2711. <u>Definition for chapter</u>

As used in this chapter -

(1) the terms defined in section 2510 of this title have, respectively, the definitions given such terms in that section; and

(2) the term "remote computing service" means the provision to the public of computer storage or processing services by means of an electronic communication system.

Source: http://www.phillipsnizer.com/library/topics/computer_fraud.cfm: accessed: 25/01/2007. A compilation by Martin Samson

2.3   Social and Ethical Issues

Although society abhors fraud and accepts that it is wrong and should be prevented. The methods that are used to detect or prevent fraud sometimes conflict with the law and also violate the right of the individual's privacy. This section examines certain factors that restrain the effective application of methods developed and devised to detect or prevent crime. **Privacy** is one of such factors. A method such as data marching of personal records compiled for unrelated purposes actually violates the data processing act 1984 that have subsequently been reviewed since 1992, 1998 and 2000. Despite that this is supported by the Act, end users have the right to control personal information and prevent its use without consent for purposes unrelated to those for which it was collected. **The due process of the law**, also makes it difficult for the individual not to be notified in a situation where data marching have taken place and has been found to fall in a category where he is possibly viewed as a potential fraudulent person. Since notifying the individual might affect the investigation, his right for justice in most instances is curtailed.

Although it might affect the course of the investigation, apprehending or arresting people on the grounds of data marching on possibly an insecure computer system mounted somewhere is ethically wrong. If we, persons of information systems management background, view this as ethically incorrect, what will be the ordinary person's view. It will certainly be seen as a humiliation and a miscarriage of justice in any form. As a result of this societal response, the security of distant funds transfer and other banking activities are sometimes crippled by this social issue, as such crimes are committed without anyone being held responsible. "Power imbalance or power in the wrong hands". This is how we term it, because too much power has been given to ordinary people to explore technology to any extent to which they desire. If there will be improvement in the security management of information then the power balance much change. Internal controls must be highly improved and co-ordinated through all banking institutions. Companies are marketing their products at the expense of information security, in view of this Governments must review policies that control the operations of businesses.

2.4   Summary

Chapter 2 discussed legal issues on Online transactions and electronic security by providing key references to independent organisations that sought the interest of consumers. References were also made to common acts of the legislature adopted globally. A compilation by Martin Samson on interpretations of internet law was presented. The chapter focused on internet law because the author believed that it was essential that stakeholders of Online Business understood the implications of internet law on Online Business since it constituted an important aspect of the legal framework.

Chapter 3

Online Business Systems

3.1   Introduction

The author believes that Online Business Systems are both Heterogeneous and Hetero-standard. This means infrastructure of these systems are supported and serviced by different service providers operating with different security and quality standards. On the contrary, most expert and non expert end users and consumers of Online Business Systems view it as heterogeneous and homo-standard. Consumers view Online Business as services from different providers, however of equal security and quality standard. In a world where electronic commerce activities transcend the walls and boundaries of every country, this cannot be the case. Due to the conflicting demands of Online Business, there is no single technology that is capable of meeting the consumer's demand. This causes the need to understand concepts underpinning heterogeneous and hetero-standard systems across global computer networks.

3.2   Heterogeneous and Hetero-Standard Systems

The term "**heterogeneous system**" in lay term refers to two or more computer or communication networks serviced or supported by different vendors that have the capability to operate and communicate using different software and hardware. The term "**hetero-standard system**" is a term coined by the author to refer communication networks that are governed by different security and quality standards. A heterogeneous system is synonymous to a distributed system. The main difference is that heterogeneity is central and a functional characteristic of a distributed system, while a distributed system comprises distributed processes and communication network. Examples are the Internet via Transport Control Protocol/Internet Protocol (TCP/IP) and Asynchronous Transfer Mode (ATM).

The infrastructure of such a heterogeneous architecture is made of middleware, operating system and of course a communication network. In a conservative sense, an operating system has middleware functionality. However, in more recent times, middleware has become an independent area of technology that drives heterogeneous systems.

3.3   Infrastructure

Online Business Systems Infrastructure mainly comprise Telephone, ISDN (Integrated Service Digital Network), VoIP (Voice over Internet Protocol), Internet, LAN (Local Area Networks), MAN (Metropolitan Area Network), WAN (Wide Area Networks), Smart Mobile Phones and Computers with WLAN, Bluetooth, Infrared, GPRS, Satellite Receivers, GPS Systems with real time data synchronisation capabilities and Database Management Systems. There are also Video Networks and IP Camera Systems for business activities and processes that require the synchronization of static and moving image transfer across a communication network. Connecting devices play a vital role within the communication infrastructure.

3.3.1   Telephone

A Telephone in simple terms is a medium that carries voice signals from one point to another. You may understand this better by conducting a primitive experiment. Take two matches or scratch boxes. Create a hole in both boxes using a sharp and pointed needle. Tie a thread at both ends at a distance of 10 meters. Attempt to communicate with another person by making that person hold the other end. You will observe that the voice signal received at the other end is audible. The thread serves as a medium carrying the voice signals in wave form at both ends.

A basic Telephone system is a communication device that consists of a handset, receiver and a twisted pair cable or wire that is usually connected to the handset. Every handset has a base station. This base station is also designed to support a cordless or wireless phone which has no direct connection to the base station. Cordless phones of such nature communicate within a 30 meter radius. A Telephone is also known as a local loop. Coaxial lines or wires connect to a local loop or pole that is usually located in the local community or resident where the communication will take place. Local loops in the residential area serve as communication links to a central office that has a more robust communication node and line capable of co-ordinating signals from local residents to other communities. The node in communication technology is called a trunk. Calls made from local residents via the trunk may be directed to other residents in the local community or channelled to a long distance service provider facilitating the calls to appropriate destinations.

Telephone systems communicate by using number allocation systems. This is common knowledge and need no mention. The numbers usually comprise an area code, an exchange number and a subscriber's extension. For example this UK number is split into three parts; +44-0208-22398.

3.3.2   Getting Familiar with Telephone Network

In general Telephone Networks comprise a Subscriber, Local exchange (LE), Public Switch Telephone Networks (PSTNs), Mobile Switching Centres (MSC), Private Branch Exchange (PBE), International Gateway Exchange (IGE), and Gateway Mobile switching Centres (GMSC). These networks are all integrated to one another in modern telephone networks as Integrated Services Digital Network (ISDN).

3.4   Integrated Services Digital Network (ISDN)

Integrated Services Digital Network provides end user access to public access networks between homes and businesses. It enables users to send fax messages, Teletext, credit card calling, call forwarding and effective answering system. ISDN provides a higher capacity data transfer compared to ordinary telephone systems and lines. Users are charged by the capacity or volume of data transfer rather than the time spent during connection. It is designed to maintain effective and more efficient public telecommunications network that support residential and business users who engage in activities such as electronic and online banking. ISDN uses complimenting technologies such as the frame relay. It ensures permanent connection dedicated for data transfer, excluding voice signals.

3.5   Local Area Network (LAN)

A local area network (LAN) is a computer or communication network that covers 100 meters radius. It is usually within a local community. Example is a computer network in a building or buildings across different parts of a local community. A LAN comprise a number of computers usually between 2 and 200 computers or more depending on how a Systems Analyst or Designer determines the physical structure and logical configuration of the network. It also comprises a thin cable called twisted pair, red copper cables known as coaxial cable, a fibre optic on some occasions, a hub or switch. The Hub or Switch is an interface device that enables the interconnection of 2 to 16 computers to form a single node. The node is analogous to the node of a tree, where one or more branches sit on a single node of that tree. Each computer is networked to another computer via what is known as a network interface card (NIC). This resides in almost every IBM standard computer. There is sometimes the use of a Bridge, a more sophisticated device that enable 8 to 36 computers to interconnect on a single node or branch on the network. A Small Medium Enterprise (SME) can use such a network to conduct its business activities using an ISDN, Frame Relay or the Internet.

3.6   Wide Area Networks (WAN)

A wide area network (WAN) is a network that covers a long distance usually more than 100 meters radius. It connects towns, cities and countries. It follows a structure similar to that of a LAN, except within it's topology it has devices that enable the interconnection of networks usually dispersed across the size of a country. Such devices include routers, bridges, repeaters, fibre optic and submarine cables used for more robust data transmission. A device such as Modem used at homes due to the use of the Internet is also used to connect computers remotely through a telephone line. In practical terms the Internet is a form of WAN which is accessible by the public. A unique feature of WAN is its ability to allow multiple computer users to share resources through a remote connection.

3.7   Internet and Voice over IP (VoIP)

The internet is a public network accessible via a network and data transmission protocol known as TCP/IP. It has become the major stream and vehicle to Online Business and electronic commerce. It is also called an IP Network.

3.7.1   Architecture of IP Networks

The TCP/IP family of communication protocols is used to support internetworking in enterprise and inter-enterprise applications. The protocols, which include the Internet Protocol (IP), the Transmission Control Protocol (TCP), the User Datagram Protocol (UDP) and other application protocols, are normally deployed in layers, with each layer responsible for a different aspect of data communication Minoli (1998).

1. The Link Layer (or Network Interface Layer)

This includes the device driver in the operating system and the corresponding network interface card in the computer. These handle all the hardware details of physically interfacing with the cable (Minoli) 1998.

2. The Network Layer (or Internet Layer)

This handles the movement of packets, such as routing, in the network. IP provides the network layer in the TCP/IP protocol suite (Minoli) 1998. It also contributes to network address translation.

3. The Transport Layer

This provides a flow of data between two end systems. The TCP/IP protocol suite has two transport protocols, Transmission Control Protocol (TCP) and the User Datagram Protocol (UDP). TCP provides a reliable connection-oriented flow of data between two hosts. Some of the functions of TCP are partitioning of data from the application layer into appropriately sized frames for the network layer below, acknowledging packets received and setting time-outs to ensure that the other end acknowledges packets that are sent. The reliable flow of data provided by TCP makes it possible for the application layer to ignore these details. UDP, on the other hand, provides a much simpler service to the application layer. It offers an unreliable connectionless data transmission service by sending packets of data called datagrams from one host to the other, but does not guarantee the delivery of the datagrams to the other end. The application layer must add any desired reliability (Minoli) 1998.

3.8   VoIP

Voice over Internet Protocol is the ability to make telephone calls and send faxes over IP-based data networks with a suitable quality of service (QoS) and superior benefit. VoIP is a new low-quality and inexpensive service. It does not match the existing phone system in terms of voice quality, reliability and security. In a similar way to other innovations, it has the potential to improve faster than its established competitor and eventually replace the existing higher-quality telephone service in the mainstream market Woabank (2000).

The immediate goal of VoIP service providers is to reproduce existing telephone capabilities at a significantly lower "total cost of production" and to offer a technically competitive alternative to (Public Switch Telephone Network) PSTN, thereby companies can reap the benefits such as reduced operational costs, improved organizational flexibility and a single network topology Woabank (2000).

Although there are reasons for the migration of Voice traffic to IP networks, there are certain problems or obstructions to be tackled, amongst them are end-to-end delays. This is one of the most important factors for the quality of interactive voice communication between two persons. When this exceeds a certain value, the interactive nature becomes more like a half-duplex communication (the listener assumes that the speaker has not yet began the conversation and begins to speak, but in the meantime the speech from the other end arrives). Another factor considered is the delay jitter, which obstructs the proper reconstruction of voice packets in their original sequential and periodical pattern; it is basically interpreted as the difference in the total end-to-end delay of two voice packets in the flow Kos (2002). There is also a Frame deletion which occurs when the IP packets carrying speech frame does not arrive to the receiver in time due to reasons considered above. The last factor is Out-of-order packet delivery, a phenomenon that occurs in the network with a complex topology of more than one path between sender and receiver Kos (2002).

The quality of services (QoS) remains a major risk factor for this technology. It was ascertained that the introduction of QoS to IP network does have effect on all four-performance measures. This can explain why network equipment manufacturers are putting high bets and hopes for the introduction of QoS mechanism into IP networks. Though there are other means to improve performance of the application, they however require real-time transmission, (Kos) 2002.

VoIP is becoming popular and widely mentioned among the user community. As a result of this, it will be appropriate to explain basic technical jargons for both technical and non technical readers.

James (2004) referred to VoIP as a means of making cheap or even free phone calls using the Internet. It takes advantage of one of the important characteristics of the Internet; that you are not charged for the distance data travels. Using VoIP means you can talk as long as you want. In fact, VoIP might not just be cheaper than the traditional phone system, it may also be superior in quality.

Users expect such connections to provide the same voice quality as the Public Switched Telephone Network (PSTN). The protocols for defining a data network were designed for non-real-time data traffic, where network congestion results in dropped packets and requests for retransmissions, Mehta (2001).

3.8.1 IP Telephony

Minoli (1998) states that IP Telephony uses a single network to carry voice and video data traffic, as a result creating a single consolidated network environment. It consists of three areas, Voice, Video and text (Fax).

Williams (2004) states that "IP (Internet Protocol) address comprises a network number and PC or host number allocated internally or externally". The internal allocation of IP address is known as a private unofficial IP address, which consists of a network and a host number. It represents the source and destination of packet information. IP is the method used to send data from one computer to another via the Internet. Every network is linked or interfaced to the Internet via a router that has an IP address. In other words a router has IP information regarding all networks linked to itself.

IP Telephony covers the technologies that use this packet-switched approach to exchange voice, video, fax and other kinds of communication,
over shared lines in a dependable flow. Previously these have been carried
using the circuit-switched connections of voice-oriented Public Switch
Telephone Networks (PSTN)'s Woabank (2000).

3.8.2   IP Telephony Technology

This section describes the technology of IP telephony, voice digitization
and compression techniques. It further describes different types of IP telephony configuration, the protocols and their standards. Voice over IP (VoIP),
also known as IP telephony is not a network, but a new application on
Internet protocol network, where voice is transported on a network that
uses circuit-switching technology. IP telephony has grown and is now becoming part of the mainstream telecom scene. All of the world's top Telecommunications organisations are exploiting IP telephony in some way,
although few are reacting to the full breadth of its impact. This section
briefly examines the operation and performance of VoIP, considering issues with its deployment and reviewing the gains and barriers of deploying
VoIP Lee (2001).

Lee et al (2001) also refers to VoIP as the next generation telephony, computer telephony integration, packet telephony, intranet and or extranet telephony, voice over the network or voice conferencing, but preferable as IP
telephony. This means the use of Internet technology to replace a long distance, or international provider of traditional telephone service, or an en-
hanced form of human-to-human communication using the computer as the
user interface rather the telephone.

On the other hand, Hart (2003) describes it as voice over data and internet
telephone service which operates by converting voice signals to data packets, sending these data packets through the internet, converting these packets back into telephone signals, and managing the overall call setup (dialup)
connection, and termination (hang-up). Hart went further to describe how
the quality of service for Internet telephone could be measured. An ordinary telephone is plugged into an adapter that connects to the broadband
setup. The call is routed over the Web to a VoIP service provider which
connects the calls to the telephone system.

The diagram in figure 6 illustrates the operation of Voice over IP

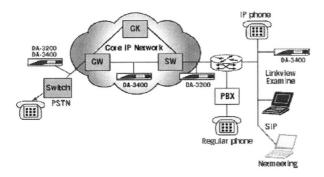

Figure 6 – Operation of Voice over IP
Source: http://www.acterna.com/images/products/2nd_level_product_pages/voip.jpg

3.8.3   Types of IP Telephony Configuration

(Lee et al 2001) analysed three important classes of Internet Telephony applications, which are:

1. Class 1-IP Terminal to IP Terminal

These are proposals with the goal of using the internet to provide plain old telephone service, telephony between existing telephone end user equipment, requiring technology for interconnection between PSTN and internet networks without the need for computer based end nodex. This configuration also requires both parties participating in the call to have a PC with software. The PC software does the compression and decompression of the data being transferred.

2. Class 2-IP Terminal to Phone or Phone to IP Terminal

These are proposals that require interoperation between the existing telephone and Internet networks, providing communications between users with either computers or existing telephone sets as end systems. This configuration requires a gateway on the edge of the IP network to translate the packets on the IP network to a suitable form for the switched circuit network. This gateway takes care of the signalling between the two networks.

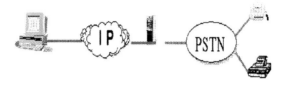

Figure 7 – IP terminal to phone
Source: (Koistinen) 1998

3. Class 3-Phone to Phone

These are proposals that use Internet – attached computers to provide some form of human communication across the packet-switched Internet. More than one gateway is required, with gateways on both ends taking care of traffic and signalling translations between networks. Here it is complete form of internet-based communication and does not involve any aspect of PSTN. It is 100% Internet and 0% PSTN.

3.9   Supporting Protocols and Standards

Protocols are the languages used for communication amongst different equipments available in IP telephony. Signalling protocols are used to set up and tear down calls, carry information required to locate users and nego-tiate capabilities. These signalling protocols are at the heart of IP telephony and distinguish it from other services. Media controlling protocols are used for controlling telephony gateways from external call control elements called media gateway controllers or call agents. Since IP telephony is still in its infancy, discussions have centred on how the protocol will bridge the legacy and next-generation networks. There are two main protocols that have taken shape: H.323 and Session Initiation Protocol (SIP). Two other protocols, which are also in use, are the Simple Gateway Control Protocol (SGCP) and the Media Gateway Control Protocol (MGCP). These will not be discussed in this section. Apart from these protocols, there are also other supporting protocols such as the Real-time Transport Protocol (RTP), the Real Time Control Protocol (RTCP), Session Description Protocol (SDP), Real Time Streaming Protocol (RTSP) and Session Announcement Proto-col (SAP). This section will describe the H.323 protocol.

3.9.1 H.323 Protocol

H.323 is an umbrella recommendation from the International telecommunications Union (ITU) that sets standards for multimedia communications over Local Area Networks (LANs). These standards do not provide a guaranteed Quality of Service (QoS). ITU's Study Group 16 approved the first version in 1996, while version 2 was approved in January 1998. The H.323 standard provides a foundation for audio, video and data communications across IP-based networks. H.323 is part of a larger series of communications standards that enable video-conferencing across a range of networks known as H.32X. This series includes H.320 and H.324, which address ISDN and PSTN communications, respectively.

The H.323 standard consists of the following components and protocols:

Feature	Protocol
Call Signalling	H.225
Media Control	H.245
Audio Codecs	G.711, G.722, G.723, G.728, G.729
Video Codecs	H.261, H.263
Data Sharing	T.120
Media Transport	RTP/RTCP

3.9.2 Architectural Overview H.323 Protocol

The H.323 recommendation covers the technical requirements for audio and video communications services in LANs that do not provide a guaranteed Quality of Service (QoS). H.323 references the T.120 specification for data conferencing. The scope of H.323 does not include the LAN itself or the transport layer that may be used to connect various LANs. Only elements needed for interaction with the Switched Circuit Network (SCN) are within the scope of H.323. Figure 8 outlines an H.323 system and its components.

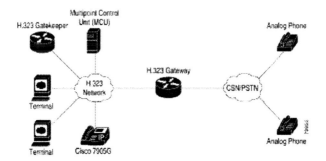

Figure 8 – Architectural overview of H.323 protocol
Source: ([Databeam)

3.9.3   H.323 Components of a Network-Based Communication System

H.323 defines four major components for a network-based communications system: Terminals, Gateways, Gatekeepers and Multipoint Control Unit (MCU).

1. Terminal

A terminal is an end point of LAN client that provides real-time, two-way communication. In VoIP all terminals must support voice communications. Video and data are optional. H.323 specifies the modes of operation required for different audio, video, and/or data terminals to work together.

All H.323 terminals must support H.245, Q.931, Registration/Admission/ Status (RASS) and Real Time Transport Protocol/Real Time Control Protocol (RTP/RTCP). H.245 is used to negotiate channel usage and capabilities and Q.931 is used for call signalling and call set-up. RASS is a protocol used to communicate with a gatekeeper while RTP/RTCP is used for sequencing audio and video packets. H.323 may also include T.120 data conferencing protocols, video codecs and MCU capabilities.

2. Gateway

The H.323 gateway is an optional element, which reflects the characteristics of a SCN endpoint, such as the PSTN, and H.323 endpoint. It is used for translation between audio, video and data transmission formats as well as communication systems and protocols. This includes call set-up and teardown on both the IP network and the SCN. Gateways are only required when there is an interconnection with the SCN. Therefore, H.323 endpoints can communicate directly over the packet network without connecting to a gateway. The gateway acts as an H.323 terminal or MCU on the network and an SCN terminal or MCU on the SCN.

3.10   Wireless and Mobile Communication Systems

Wireless and mobile communication systems support customer service applications such as emails, directory services, internet browsing, search activities and many more.

It is advocated by some researchers that wireless communication systems took root in late 70's and early 80's with the introduction of (AMPS) Advanced Mobile Phone System introduced by AT&T of USA. This was an analogue system that used frequency modulation to transmit conversation through wireless medium. This development was superseded by (GSM) Global System for Mobile Communication. Glenn et al (1999).

Other developments that support modern Online Business include (TDMA) Time Division Multiple Access and (CDMA) Code Division Multiple Access. In CDMA the consumer is allocated a code which enables spreading of transmission signals across allocated spectrum on the network. It has been chosen as the multiple signalling format for 3rd generation mobile systems Gu X, Dodds S.J (2006). It is also designed to provide additional services such as high data rate transmission and multimedia data transfer. (DS/CDMA) Direct Sequence Code Division Multiple Access is designed for broadband wireless systems. The medium access control layer protocol for communication is known as "slotted Aloha" Gu X, Dodds S.J (2006). TDMA allocates time slot within the wireless spectrum to the consumer from beginning to the end of a conversation. In (FDMA) Frequency Division Multiple Access Channel, a channel within a frequency is allocated to the consumer. Among the technologies mentioned so far, GSM has the widest coverage and consumer market. The consumer or subscriber can communicate with the mobile phone almost across the globe via a roaming service. Global communication has been effective using wireless satellite systems. Most Online business activities are mainly supported by satellite systems.

3.10.1   Basic Concepts in Wireless Systems

A basic wireless communication system comprises a wireless router that serves as an access point to the wireless network via a computer with an in-built or plug-in wireless adapter or card. The wireless system can consist of devices such as smart phones and infrared devices or sensors.

3.10.2   Wireless Communication Standards and Protocols

A communication standard is the agreed data format for communication, whiles a communication protocol specifies the rules underlying the communication format. Wireless communication standards and protocols support local area communication networks as well as global communication networks. This is achieved through protocols and standards such as (WDP) Wireless Datagram Protocol, (WAP) Wireless Application Protocol gateway, Bluetooth, WLAN, WiFi, and WiMax and Satellite. These protocols play a key role in wireless communication systems. Other forms of wireless technology supporting mobility in Business and Commerce include the application of infrared systems, sensor and energy constraint networks. Authentication protocols that support these systems include Wired Equivalent Privacy (WEP), Medium Access Control (MAC) Filtering, RADIUS, Kerberos and (WTLS) Wireless Transport Layer Security.

3.10.3   Wireless Local Area Networks (WLAN) Standards

Wireless Local Area Networks (WLAN) use infrared and radio frequency signals to communicate. These technologies are both part of the (IEEE) Institute of Electrical and Electronic Engineers 802.11 Wireless LANs standard. The infrared and radio frequency signals are part of the physical layer of any WLAN architecture. WLAN supports mobile and portable devices for home, small businesses, enterprises and accessible public areas. Sections 3.5.3.1 to 3.5.3.2 outline common standards that support wireless local area networks.

3.10.3.1 IEEE 802.1x

This identifies and specifies the source of a connection to an entry point or port of a communication network. There is an authentication service performed for remote connection to the network. It is a specification of a protocol for data transmission amongst different network nodes. It also links an authenticator and the authentication service of the network

3.10.3.2 IEEE 802.11

Bluetooth and Handheld devices – An Ad hoc network standard which allows the dynamic connection of remote devices such as mobile telephones, laptops and PDAs. This standard is designed for connections designed for non fixed network infrastructure. It supports 1 to 2Mbps data transmission. Subsets of the standard include the following:

- **802.11a** - High speed WLAN that transmits within 5 GHz band.

- **802.11b** - WLAN standard for 2.4 GHz band. Has a data link rate of 11Mbps per channel, throughput of 2.5-4Mbps.

- **802.11d** - A roaming standard that supports medium access control of a network. This standard is not deployed in part of the globe.

- **802.11e** - Supports quality of service.

- **802.11f** - Defines inter-access communication point and multi splendour authentication.

- **802.11g** - This is physical layer standard for WLAN. Use additional modulation between 2.4 to 2.4835 GHz bands. Maximum link rate is 54Mbps for every channel.

- **802.11h** - This standard provides support for the MAC layer for 5Ghz banport level transmission.

☐ **802.11i** - Provides a better security than the (WEP) Wired equivalent privacy, more robust encryption standards such as AES 3DES.

☐ **802.11n** - Provides speed to 500Mbps.

☐ **802.1x** – This standard is for port access and authentication.

3.10.4   Satellite Systems

A satellite communication system comprises a radio transmitter in a space station, transponder, a dish, set of antennas and an earthlink or station. Satellites are located in Orbit which is either geostationary or geosynchronous. Satellite systems support devices such as cell or mobile phones, i-PaQs or PDAs. Whiles wireless standards and protocols such as WLAN provide users and consumers access to the internet, satellites have the capability to do the same on a global platform Chartrand, Mark R (2004).

3.10.4.1 Satellite Systems, Standards and Service Groups

Satellite systems and standards include NTSC (National Television Standards Committee), SECAM (Sequential Colour with Memory), and PAL (Phase Alteration by Line) used in some parts of Europe. Six common service groups of satellite communication are; FSS (Fixed Satellite Service), BSS (Broadcast Satellite Service, MSS (Mobile Satellite Service), RDSS (Radio Determination Satellite Service), RNSS (Radio Navigation Satellite Service) and ISS (Inter-Satellite Service) Chartrand, Mark R (2004).

3.10.4.2 Satellite Applications and Services

The type of services satellite systems support includes synchronisation of distributed data on the internet, pay per view television services and broadcast. They also serve as a vehicle for placing telephone calls, making a video broadcast or video conference. Signals are usually transmitted from consumers to earth stations using wired media such as coaxial cables and fibre optic links. Other application areas are audio for radios and music to i-Pod, in-flight entertainment on aeroplanes. A more recent application available to consumers is satellite navigation systems for vehicles using Global Positioning System (GPS). A technology useful for location based services, remote sensing and control.

A GPS is a system consisting of approximately 24 navigation star satellites in a 12 hour medium altitude Orbit within a number of planes. Signal transmission is time based. This means that signal transmission should be within exact intervals. Users usually receive signals, but cannot transmit from their receivers. In order for a user's location or position to be accurate, information received should originate from a synchronised set of satellites. GPS function between 1.57542GHz and 1.22760 GHz frequencies. Satellites also support Online Businesses in supply chain management. Many companies distribute data via LAN, WAN and Internet. The data distributed may be about a product or service information. In Stock Management and Inventory Control, Satellite Communication could be a very useful technology for data sharing and matching. This is common in B2C and B2B environments and useful for Businesses which want to provide logistical support to Clients via seamless communication channels. Delivery management in B2B applications among super markets and chain stores is vital if not a critical success factor. Super chain stores also implement Electronic Point of Sale System (EPOS) hooked unto an inventory system known as V-SAT. A cross section of internet communication is powered by satellite technology.

3.10.5 Infrared Systems

Infrared is a form of light wave that is invisible to the human eye. It falls within the general spectrum of light, which is commonly described as the Electromagnetic Spectrum (EMS). This EMS comprise light waves. The waves include microwave, ultra-violet, gama rays, x-rays and near infrared. There are technological devices at cutting edge that use infrared light wave to communicate among devices. For example, mobile phones, Laptops, i-paqs (pocket computers), cameras, pen drives etc. Online Business is facilitated and driven by such devices that have the capability to communicate on a network platform through infrared ray or light wave. From an end user's perspective an infrared transmission is perceived as a form of wireless communication. It has a wavelength between (-1) and (1) micrometer. An infrared using imaging technique has a colour which is at the edges of the colours of rainbow. The imaging is usually captured via the properties of light such as the wavelength, frequency and energy of the wave signal. Applications of Infrared include data transfer from a phone to computer or Laptop. It can also be used by cameras for night vision, and for purposes of ubiquitous computing Deremiak E.L and Boreman G.D (1996).

3.11   Summary

Chapter 3 was an overview and review of Online Business Systems. The author believes that Online Business Systems are both Heterogeneous and Hetero-standard. The term "Heterogeneous system" in lay term refers to two or more computers or communication networks services by different vendors. These vendors have the capability to operate and communicate using different hardware and software. "Hetero-standard system" refers to communication networks governed by different security or quality standards. Infrastructure formed the nucleus of Online Business Systems. The infrastructure reviewed included; Telephone, Integrated Service Digital Network (ISDN), Local Area Network (LAN), Wide Area Network (WAN), Voice Over IP (VoIP), architecture of IP Networks, overview of IP Telephony and associated configuration. There was emphasis on wireless and mobile communication systems such as infra red systems, satellite communication, Bluetooth and WLAN.

Chapter 4

Online Business Security Technologies

4.1 Introduction

This chapter examines Online Business Security Technologies. The chapter examines security standards and protocols such as SET, SSL and IPSEC. The chapter explains the role of Virtual Private Networks in Online Business transactions. The role of crypto-systems in security is also explained. New trends in authentication are introduced, whiles common models such as PPP, CHAP, Kerberos and Biometrics are also re-examined.

4.2 Security Standards and Protocols

"A standard is a document established by consensus and approved by a recognised body which provides, for common and repeated use, rules, guidelines or characteristics for activities or their results, aimed at the achievement of optimum degree of order in a given context" ISO/IEC Guide 2 (1996).

It is also a document that ensures uniformity, consistency, openness and global participation in the advancement of technology through set rules and guidelines Williams (2004). Whiles standards ensure uniformity, openness and global participation, Protocols serve as rules that govern the implementation of standards.

The subject of online payment technology is paramount and central to electronic commerce and business applications. The role of credit cards, such as its applications in mail and telephone ordering, face to face exchange and the role of the Internet in online transactions is pivotal to the current climate of freedom economy. Security standards and protocols including SSL, SET, and IPSEC contribute to the drivers of cyber commerce. These technologies are central to the security and success of credit card payments. The other forms of e-payment systems central to cyber commerce and Online Business include digital cash and cheque, debit cards, smart cards, store and loyalty cards, prepaid, telephone and micro payments systems.

Although there have been much emphasis on online payment systems and security methods, vulnerability assessment is not adequately performed on these systems. Security is important to clients who use payment technologies and systems, although most users and consumers of these online systems are quite naïve about the value of information and associated asset being protected. It is also true that they are not fully aware of their state of vulnerability. More recently, mobile payments and wireless systems are also beginning to play a key role in Online Business.

It is also becoming a subject of critical importance to on-going technological agenda within academia and industry. This is also expressed in the works of Keen and Mackintosh (2001). Software agents are also growing in popularity within the online auction market, for example e-bay uses agent applications for searching bargains on the Internet for customers. Software agents, in lay terms, perform useful services on behalf of customers who surf the Internet or search online auction market generic services. Examples of such services are naming and directory services. For instance, Google search engine applies efficient and intelligent techniques in data search and retrieval which is tailored to respond to customer and client needs. This can be further explored in the book "Google Legacy" Arnolds S (2005).

Agnew, Wong, Mirlas, Kou and Lin (2003) present concepts and issues affecting secure electronic transactions (SET), a standard drawn from contributions made from VISA and Master card. In general security protocols deployed as part of the TCP/IP protocol suite, include IPsec, SSL and SET. IPsec is implemented at the network layer. Although contents are usually protected, there are issues with traceability of source and destination data. This could be a form of vulnerability. IPsec can also encrypt a standard message and subsequently place this message in a disguised header. This technique is known as tunnel mode. This permits users to set up private groups over networks, usually in the form of VPNs (Virtual Private Networks). There are also difficulties in authenticating individual users, since IP addresses could be shared on a network. Even though SSL has its strengths, recent developments reveal key vulnerabilities. This is because it provides only transport level security.

Most security vulnerabilities originate from the network layer. Also see Synchronizing E-Security for more information on vulnerability spots on networks Williams (2003). This might serve as a loop hole if there is no robust security at the network layer. Complimenting this is application layer security. SET is a form of application layer security standard that relies more on digital certificates. Certificates sometimes have trust issues with them. The subsequent paragraphs provide an outline of SET. Robustness is a key strength of SET, it however has performance related problems.

SSL lacks effective mutual authentication which is critical to security of electronic commerce transactions. Section 4.3 discusses these standards in more detail.

4.3   Managing the Implementation of Standards

The role of standards and its implementation has caused the need to enforce section 404 of Sarbanes Oxley (SOX) Act as a means of ensuring compliance and control of ICT systems and infrastructure. SOX places importance on the auditing of ICT systems and associated business processes. It makes executives to be directly responsible for ensuring that appropriate controls are implemented across every level of the organisation. The implementation of controls within organisations is integral, if not central to the management of risk and security associated with ICT infrastructure. Although most organisations and businesses have some form of ICT control system designed to enforce security, they are not always rigorous and adequate. ICT management personnel and systems should support key areas by playing the following roles in accordance with ICT control objectives for SOX:

- Understand the organisation's internal control program and its financial reporting.
- Map ICT systems that support internal control to financial reporting process to the financial statements.
- Identify risks related to these systems.
- Design and implement controls designed to mitigate risks identified and monitoring them for continuous effectiveness.
- Document and test ICT controls Ensure that ICT controls are updated and changes as necessary to correspond with changes in internal control and reporting process.
- Participation by ICT in the management of SOX.

Control should cut across areas such as computer operations, data and program access, program development and change.

Source *IT control objectives for SOX 2nd Edition. Exposure draft 2006. Standards that could be implemented in conjunction with SOX include;*

- ISO/IEC 17799: 2005 – Code of practice for information security management usually mapped unto COBIT.

Table 1 – 11 domain areas of ISO17799-2005

No.	Domain name	Sub domain	
1	Security Policy	N/A	
2	Organizational information security	4	Information security infrastructure
		5	Security of third party access
		6	Outsourcing
3	Asset management	•	Accountability of assets
		•	Information classification
4	Personnel Security & Human resources security	•	Security in Job definition and resource management
		•	User training
		•	Responding to security incidents/malfunctions
5	Physical and environment security	•	Secure areas
		•	Equipment security
		•	General controls
6	Communications and operations management	•	Operational procedures and responsibilities
		•	System planning and acceptance
		•	Protection against malicious programs
		•	House keeping
		•	Network management
		•	Media handling and security
		•	Exchange of information and software
7	Access control	•	Business requirement for access control
		•	User access management
		•	User responsibilities
		•	Network access control
		•	Operating system access Control
		•	Application access control
		•	Monitoring system access and use
		•	Mobile computing and Tele working
8	Information system development, acquisition and maintenance	•	Security requirement of systems
		•	Security in application systems
		•	Cryptography controls
		•	Security of system files
		•	Security development and support processes
9	Information security incident management	N/A	
10	Business continuity Management	N/A	
11	Compliance	•	Compliance with legal requirements
		•	Review of security Policy and compliance

Table 1 is an outline of the 11 domain areas that provide the framework for best code of practice for information security management. It is highly recommended that any information security system implemented should be benchmarked against this standard. There are other forms of standards that ensure that other aspects of system requirements are addressed at the appropriate level Singleton T.W (2006). These standards include;

ISACA – Volume 1 2006, Tommie W. Singleton, COBIT – A key to success as an ICT auditor.

☐ COBIT – Effective for ICT governance and control framework. Whiles COBIT3 focuses on how to implement controls COBIT4 focuses on what to do of control. There is emphasis on good practice, which revolves on standards.

☐ ISO21188 – A public key infrastructure (PKI) standard that ensures security of financial transactions on the Internet. It is designed to protect online transactions from identity theft, intrusion attacks and cyber crime. It provides a set of guidelines designed to assist security and audit managers, business directors in the financial sector.

☐ ITIL – This is the Information Technology Infrastructure Library (ITIL) developed by the UK office of Government Commerce. It is a source of reference for IT service management. It is effective for ICT auditing and can be mapped unto other best practice standards such as COBIT, ISO17799 and BS1500.

☐ ISO/IEC TR-13335 – Guidelines for the management of ICT security (technical guidelines).

- □ NIST 800-14 - Accepted principles and practices for securing ICT systems.

- □ COSO – Applied for internal control that is mapped unto COBIT.

- □ CMMI – Capability Maturity Model Integration (CMMI), best practice for improving processes.

- □ FIPS – USA federal information processing standards pub. 200. Minimum security requirement for federal information systems.

Adopting best practice standards have several benefits, in online business, such as;

- □ Increase in confidence and trust among customers.

- □ Effective security implementation.

- □ Sustenance of business operations and processes.

- □ Long term cost reduction in training and modalities for exceptional control.

- □ Benchmark for companies' performance.

- □ Improvement in auditing of information systems by meeting basic industry requirements.

4.3.1   Designing Standards and Policies

Standards designed to ensure the management of effective security technologies and systems for electronic transactions in a global economy need to be critically assessed. Until recently customers had to queue at counters in order to withdraw money, cash their cheques and transfer funds. The use of sophisticated technology in the banking sector and other financial service companies has enabled us to enjoy Online banking service in the comfort of our homes and work places. This has been made possible as a result of e-government policies Gonzi (2001). It is important to bear in mind that information security management as an issue, is an international one. This is because although Governments are keen in getting the problem improved, the approach adopted by advanced economies towards policies and standards of implementation excludes countries which are less developed. It is the writer's opinion and belief that a joint international consultation is needed to reach a consensus on policies and standards. International consensus means international security support. What it actually implies is that policies and standards, covering information security, must not be derived by only the giants in technology, such as Japan, America or UK Williams (2004).

Lord Renwick former Chairman of the IMIS (Institute for the Management of Information Systems) political advisory committee in UK on 22nd October 1997 opened a short debate on electronic commerce asking her Majesty's government "What steps Government intended to take to ensure the city of London remained the leading centre for world-wide electronic trade in the face of United States government initiatives intended to ensure that internet-based commerce is conducted under US security standards" Campbell (1997)?

"In the introductory analysis it was mentioned that national policies and standards derived and proposed as international standards and policies were unlikely to work in the long term. How could one or two countries solve an issue that needs global participation and co-operation? The open remarks by Lord Renwick during the debate on such an issue of global concern defeated the purpose it was intended to achieve. Although Lord Renwick set the "ball rolling" by asking such a provocative and thought challenging question, the end result of such a debate was to determine policies and standards, which were to be formulated to guide the future of information security management in the UK" Williams (2003). Recapturing the introduction of the debate, quoting Lord Renwick, "We hear much talk of the global information society of the future and appear to assume that the language will be American, the cultural values those of Hollywood and the legal values of Perry Mason." It is not clear what these remarks meant, whether he made them because America had taken the initiative to set standards and policies which were supposedly going to govern the security management of electronic trade world wide, without UK taking the lead in policies and standards or he had the rest of the world in mind. If the presumption made here is right, then he equally advocated and supported the notion in the debate that setting of policies and standards must be approached on an international platform. Although approaching the setting of policies and standards from the basis and perception of leaders in the development of the technology is not completely wrong, such a regional approach must only be designed by all interest groups world wide and subsequently submitted to an international forum for discussion.

Adopting a guideline such as (ISO17799) is a way of ensuring that the required standards are upheld. This ensures that security breaches are prevented. This is because it has already earned international recognition and acceptance as a very productive way forward to ensuring information systems process certification. Organisations can have their implementation of the ISO17799 evaluated and certified under any accredited certification scheme. Standards driven by more advanced economies with almost no involvement of developing economies are unlikely to succeed, given e-commerce and Online Business have now become a global agenda. The design of international policies and its influence on developing economies is insignificant. This is due to the fact that developing economies adopt international security standards that are already packaged.

4.4   Security Systems and Technologies

4.4.1   Secure Electronic Transactions (SET)

Secure Electronic Transaction (SET) is a system for ensuring security of financial transactions on the Internet. It is also a standard designed to support the security of credit and electronic card transactions on public networks such as the Internet. Transactions are verified using digital certificates. SET uses SSL, Microsoft Secure Transaction Technology (MSTT), and Secure Hypertext Transfer Protocol (SHTTP). It also applies some aspects of Public Key Infrastructure (PKI) discussed in subsequent sections.

4.4.2   Virtual Private Networks (VPN)

VPN is a tunnel created through a public network (Internet) that carries encrypted data via the network. Business to Business (B2B) communications usually uses this form of network to ensure that integrity and confidentiality of data sent across the businesses involved in the transaction and commercial activity is protected. Businesses use VPN due to its cost effectiveness. Prior to VPN two or more organisations who wanted to do business had to setup a wide area network (WAN) as a means of ensuring security of data sent to the respective locations of these organisation. The common attacks that VPN attempts to prevent include spoofing, session hijacking of a network device such as the firewall. Some other attacks are eavesdropping or sniffing, man in the middle attack and brute force. Refer to chapters five and six for the descriptions and explanations of these attacks. The main requirements of a VPN implementation is a VPN Client and Server and a tunnel that connects the client and server in front of a firewall. See example in figure 9.

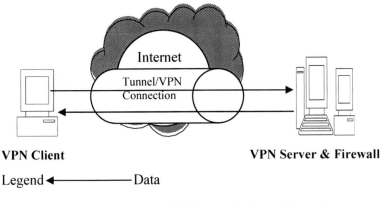

VPN Client   **VPN Server & Firewall**

Legend ◄─────────Data

Figure 9 – VPN server in front of firewall

The encryption of the tunnel could be implemented by using protocols such as IPSEC, PPP and SSL.

4.4.3   IP Security (IPSEC)

IP security commonly known as IPSec is a protocol designed to primarily provide security at the network layer of the TCP/IP protocol suite. It is used to enable private communication and data transfer on public networks such as the Internet with the sole aim of making the communication secure. It is an open standard that could be deployed in conjunction with other open standards. It is usually used to create a virtual private network (VPN). VPN implementation improves authentication and the prevention of denial of service (DOS) and replay attacks. This is because the connection is secured and insulated from the public domain. IPsec consist of the following elements:

1. A set of two security protocols, known as Authentication Header (AH) and Encapsulating Security Payload (ESP).

2. The Internet Key Exchange (IKE) protocol IPsec uses IKE to negotiate IPsec connection configuration. It provides end point authentication; set up security parameters, manage key distribution and communication channels.

3. IP Payload compression protocol for packet compression prior to encryption.

There are 3 basic VPN models implemented using IPsec. These are; Gateway to Gateway, Host to gateway and host to host.

Gateway to Gateway – implementation protects inter-network communication and ensures the security of data transmitted. This could be business to business connections B2B or Internet Service Provider ISP to ISP.

Host to Host – A tunnel implementation that protects two interconnected computers. This could be a set of nested clients or servers.

Gateway to Host – This is connection between a network and a home computer or single client.

4.4.4   Secure Socket Layer (SSL)

Secure socket layer is a protocol applied to secure the transport layer of the TCP/IP protocol. Its application supports inter and intra-website communication. SSL uses asymmetric cryptography to encrypt data transferred across a network. One key is used to encrypt while another is used to decrypt. These keys are known as private and public keys. The public key encrypts whiles the private key decrypts Keys are deployed in the form of digital certificates for purposes of key exchange and authentication.

Authentication is at client and server levels. Although SSL intends to provide confidentiality and integrity services using Data Encryption Standard (DES) algorithm, it has its own embedded weaknesses.

Below are processes that highlight how SSL works.

- Let us assume a costumer make a request from a website, which has SSL implemented, with the Uniform Resource Locator (URL) http://www.godfried.com it is initiated as a secure login request https:\\godfriedserver.com\data
- The server sends X.509 certificate containing server's public key
- Customer authenticates certificate against a list of known certificates from certification authorities
- Data is encrypted using a public key
- The encrypted data known as a cyphertext is decrypted using a private key.

Since SSL is more dependent on trust as compared to other security systems, it becomes more vulnerable to the man in the middle attack. This is because the customer/Client request should have a high level of confidence in the certificate issued or the certification authority. If we were to base our analysis on this assumption, it will imply that a certificate which is faked will be difficult to detect. From a more technical point of view, the socket layer comprises a port number and an IP address, which functions at the transport layer. The dynamic allocation of IP addresses and the ability to scan ports serve as vulnerability elements and key security concerns. There are also issues associated with key distribution with particular emphasis on the key distribution database IBM (2004).

4.5   Encryption and Online Security

It is vital to note that the art and science of cryptography provide support to data confidentiality, integrity and availability. There is significance placed on the common algorithms applied in business and commerce world that employ cryptography based systems. This intricacy is relevant for understanding the issues associated in ensuring that data which traverse across networks that support electronic commerce and business are secured. Most common algorithms include DES, 3DES, AES, RSA and Diffie-Hellman public key distribution scheme. These form the caucus of technologies required for ensuring privacy and protection of data.

4.5.1   DES, 3DES and AES

DES is an acronym for Data Encryption Standard. It is a crypto algorithm and standard that uses symmetric or same encryption and distribution keys for converting plaintext to cipher-text. The key length of DES is 56 bit. In the mid 90's DES became weak and unreliable as a crypto algorithm. It was broken using a computer with reasonable computational strength. The technique for breaking the key is known as brute force or in-depth key search.

3DES also known as triple DES. It is a derivative of DES. It uses double encryption and single decryption. It has embedded weakness which was inherited from DES. New developments in encryption standard has led to AES (Advanced Encryption Standard). Although there are a number of algorithms considered to be AES, Rijndael algorithm is federal information processing standard for AES. Rijndael has key length ranging from 128, 192 and 256 bits. One of the main reasons why Rijndael has become an AES defacto standard is based on reasons such as its capability to handle non-linearity among bits and efficiency of computer memory use Onwubiko C (2006).

4.5.2   Encryption and Authentication

Authentication is equally crucial and essential in Online Business as discussed in Williams (2003). Issues related to authentication of e-commerce activities could enlighten both technical and non technical people respectively regardless of their interest in the subject matter. This could serve as a catalyst in transforming their understanding and appreciation of the issues involved. This is based on the notion that end users seem to lack interest in technical intricacies, although this could vary from one case to another.

Server security is equally important in Online Business security modelling, a view shared by other authors, and researchers in this field. Confidentiality, Integrity, Availability, Non repudiation, Authentication, Audit and third party systems are required to facilitate electronic commerce transactions.

According to Zhang and Wang (2003), the history and background of the science and art of cryptography dates back as far as 1900 BC in the days of circa, when it was mainly used for armed forces purposes. Trust, access control and corporate security ensure some level of integrity, although that was not the original purpose of the science and art. The different forms of crypt-analysis provide useful insights to the meaning of cipher text and protected data, and the problems caused when confidentiality of data, becomes compromised. Attacks such as plain text attacks, chosen plain text attack, known plaintext attack, man in the middle attack, correlation against hardware and faults in crypto-systems are issues that need to be addressed. Quantum computing is a research area related to polynomials and discrete logarithms that could contribute solutions to Online Business problems. It is, however, not in a matured stage. DNA computing is also being developed to address crypto systems implemented globally on Online Business Systems.

4.5.3   New Trends in Authentication

Authentication is more comprehensive and effective when it is bi-directional. This means that, authentication should not only focus on consumers, but also ensure that systems which provide services for consumers are themselves authentic. One of the goals of authentication is to establish trust between customers and service providers. For Online systems, one will need to ensure that two main conditions are met. The first is the genuineness and legitimacy of the Service Provider whiles the second is genuineness of consumers who are Online. The communication media and systems in which authentication takes place are usually the Telephone, Internet via the Web, Mobile devices, reviewed in chapter 3. This section's analysis is based on the Internet (Web). For any online transaction to be authentic, the following questions should be answered satisfactorily; Are we as Service Providers dealing with the right customer? Is the alleged customer the rightful credit or debit card owner? Am I dealing with the right Bank? Is this person the right customer of the Bank? Can signs on the website be verified for authenticity? How do we know that a call from Barclays Bank, HSBC or First American Bank truly came from any of these Banks?

These are some common authentication questions that have to be verified and answered. Nine out of ten customers will not verify the authenticity of a call from a Service Provider, whether it be a Bank, Credit Card provider or utility Company.

There are new developments along the lines of application security. Web browsers are playing an important role in advancing web security and online services. Internet Explorer 7 seems to be determined in solving some of the authentication issues highlighted. The main problem associated with the authentication of websites, is the fact that the entire site could be phished. Although there are security developments to solve the problem of phishing, they are still not advanced enough to deal with current threats. One of the proposed models is to prevent copying and duplication of the Logos of Companies from their websites. Currently 90% of Logos on web-sites could be copied. Phishing, pharming and web profiling attacks render Domain name, verification of trust marks non effective when authenticating an internet site to a customer or consumer. The consumer is usually authen-ticated using address, personal details, password, and date of birth, first and last digits of the date of birth of the customer. This is common when the transaction is via phone. For bank account verification, service providers systems will ask user names and passwords. The examples provided are common to Lloyds TSB, Barclays and Alliance and Leicester Banks all operating internationally and the UK. In order for Online Business systems to sustain itself in the long term, the author believes that such systems should win consumer's confidence. This in the long term builds a trust rela-tion that is unwavering.

There are many models for authentication. These include; Traditional au-thentication systems, closed user group trusted 3rd party, Open user group trusted party (VIP), EMV CAP usually for banking applications, Hybrid (EMV CAP and VIP). There is also a review of Kerberos, Point to Point (PPP) authentication and Challenge Handshake Authentication Protocol (CHAP).

4.5.4   Authentication Methods and Online Business

This section classifies authentication into three categories, namely human to human, human to system and system to system. The author has described them as user authentication and system authentication. The reason for these three categories is based on the premise that authentication is a multidirec-tional or multidimensional activity.

The purpose of this section is to present the reader with the most common methods applied and current trends in authentication methods and how each affects the transactions we make through electronic means

Table 2 – Categories of authentication methods applied in Online Business

Types of Authentication	Human to Human	Human to System	System to System
Mutual Authentication	√	√	
Digital Certificates	√	√	√
User Identification and names		√	
Passwords		√	
Profiling		√	
Biometrics		√	
Token allocation			√
CHAP (Challenge Handshake Authentication Protocol)			√
Kerberos			√
Intelligent Agents			√
VIP – Two Factor Authentication			√

Human to Human Authentications

Human in this context refers to person, group of people and organisations. This section discusses mutual authentication and digital certificates as aspects of human to human authentication.

Mutual Authentication

This is when two people or a person and a system engage in an electronic communication in order to verify the identity of the other. An example that shows person to person or person to system is the customer and bank relationship. A clerk at the bank will ensure that a customer possesses identification, which is consistent with the information held about the customer by the bank. This information could either be the date of birth or mother's maiden name. The other example is a customer who interacts with an automated system by telephone or Internet to confirm unique personal details before the system grants approval and access to, for instance current balance.

Electronic Banking Standards and Mutual Authentication

Appropriate banking standards, especially international banking does not allow any form of transfer of funds to be carried by telephone; however these standards do not apply fully when it comes to transfer by the internet. The problem associated with this form of authentication is a challenging one. This is because persons at remote geographical locations crossing national boundaries with personal details of an electronic crime victim, could without any sweat transfer funds from one account to another. Although there are numerous computer security fraternities with computer experts, it is generally believed that there are sceptics amongst these groups when it comes to transacting any form of business on the Internet, especially when the business is across the Atlantic or Pacific. The reasons for this are mainly technical. One wonders how many switches and gateways credit card details might travel through in order for it to arrive at the appropriate destination or recipient.

Issues with Encryption

Though personal details sent across the Internet are encrypted, encryption could either be end to end or link to link encryption. The end to end encryption is commonly used since it is cheaper, while link to link encryption is rarely used because it is very expensive. The logical conclusion to draw here is that most companies will adopt the former since companies are very particular of how funds are spent and disbursed. Making profit is higher on the agenda than maximising productivity. It will be an illusion and self deception if we think otherwise. Confidentiality and integrity becomes a hurdle difficult to surmount due to the security layers that data must travel before arriving at its final destination. The layers the Information travel through are dynamic and not static.

The dynamic routing of information is considered because service providers will like to optimise the efficiency of their business transactions, therefore there is a trade off between efficiency and security, since the less congested routes on the Internet might not be secured. This implies that personal details from credit cards in the form of information packets could be sniffed or eavesdropped from the internet using for instance specialised sniffing software in the form of intelligent agents.

Effects of Poor Encryption Procedures

Absence of comprehensive encryption procedures and policies could enable an eavesdropper to sniff data from the Internet. This could be useful source of information to make a fraudulent or disrupt an Internet transaction. This is usually carried by adopting the profile of the victim whose data were eavesdropped. Pro Internet security gurus might disagree with this assertion. However, it is believed undoubtedly that there are security flaws when it comes to ensuring the integrity and confidentiality of credit card details sent across the Internet. Experts in credit card security admit that there are still major lapses in credit card security, although there has been a migration from magnetic strip to the magnetic chip. The main reasons are that although credit card embedded magnetic Chips are more secured, the cost of implementing the technology is more expensive, as a result slowing down the process of its global adaptation. The conclusion drawn is that since the total cost of security flaws is less than implementing this technology, it is more appropriate and sustainable to maintain the current technology.

Using Digital Certificates

These are used in the authentication of a person's or an organisation's digital identity during an electronic transaction. This could be used during the sending of emails or an electronic fund transfer. This again is usually combined with cryptography technologies such as encryption and digital signatures. It is mostly between individuals or organisations; however it is effectively implemented by the inclusion of a third party who confirms the legitimacy of the parties involved. There is an issue of trust when it comes to certification. This is discussed in more detail in chapter 3 under the subheading policies and standards.

(HSA) Human to System Authentication

A system here refers to the hardware, software and process components of a computer and its processing environment. This section discusses the use of user identification and names, passwords, profiling and biometrics as methods of authentication.

- **User Naming and Identification**

This is a unique identification used by humans to identify them to personal computers, computer networks and multiple networks or distributed platforms. It could be in any form; however, it is more logical to use names that have some personal relation to the user of that system. The common form of username is the first name of the user. It could also be some family related name or a nickname. It is important to realise that it is part of the authentication process and should be accorded some degree of importance as any form of authentication. User names and identifications should not be publicly accessible or seen by third parties. Making them accessible by other unauthorised persons weakens the processes of authentication in the layers of security Williams (2003).

The obtaining of user names and identification by unauthorised persons is one step forward in adopting a victim's profile. It provides a basis for masquerading. Masquerading is when one entity pretends to be a different entity Stallings (2003). This form of Masquerading could take place in the banking environment. Unauthorised users could informally attain details of customers' profile and use it for criminal activities. This is discussed in detail in the next section. Another example is enabling a member of staff of an organisation with limited database rights to obtain additional access rights by impersonating another member of staff with special administrative rights.

- **Password**

This is a series of characters when combined with a username or identification code authenticates the user of a system Williams (2004).

- **How do Password Systems Work?**

Password systems have different authentication mechanisms. They are made of algorithms that convert plaintext to another text known as cipher during encryption. This text can only be revealed using a key. A password authentication system also has a file which stores encrypted passwords of legitimate users of a system. When a user enters a password on a system, it is matched with ciphers stored in the authentication file. If the user's cipher matches with an existing cipher in the file, the user is granted access to the system. In general there are authentication protocols that support password systems. These protocols do not enforce encryption of plaintext.

- **Shortfalls of Passwords**

A password should be handled with high importance. An effective security system will encourage users to change passwords periodically through email reminders and sometimes text messages from mobile phones. This is because passwords could be deduced using probabilities and profiling techniques. For instance, a person with very deep interest in religious matters is likely to use adjectives and nouns such as holy, law, love, prophet, preacher and many more similar jargons. A politically minded person might use words like justice, election, government, policy or vote. This is at the primary stage. A secondary stage will be a combination of these words and some form of pneumonic. In fact most organisations password policies provide indication of what sought of characters are allowed. This is a give away, since it provides a hacker with adequate information to hack into a system using techniques such as dictionary attacks.

Certain users of Online Business Systems adopt passwords that depict the direct opposite of their interest. It should be understood here that, password systems as a means of authentication are not only applied in the context of Human Computer Interactions. Most banks demand a form of password or code when a customer attempts to withdraw funds at the counter. The password system is normally based on a set of routine or generic questions such as, mother's maiden name, work telephone number, home telephone number, type of personal bank card, previous home address, post code etc. These seem to be the commonest questions that are asked by most national and international banks. Such password systems are easily to break because the banks rarely implement a policy that informs the customer to make changes to password systems that match with their profile. This type of authentication process and concept is usually transferred to Internet banking in an automated form.

The probability of such systems being broken into is very high. Intruders and hackers do not need the mind of a genius to violate the security of such systems. This is because such personal information is not difficult to acquire. Information for violating password systems could be acquired through the following channels: Grapevine (informal channels of communication), advance search and queries on the Internet, Search in Garbage cans, bins in residential areas, through fake sales representative and provision of incentives to people during data collection exercises Williams (2003). The prudent security strategy is for banks to change such a system of personal profiles which is semi-permanent and unlikely to change. For example my mother's maiden name cannot be changed. My work place number is available to students for reference purposes during placement or when looking for a Job upon graduation.

System to System Authentication (SSA)

- **(CHAP) Challenge Handshake Authentication Protocol**

CHAP is a Point to Point Protocol (PPP). The objective of CHAP is to ensure that end to end systems that communicate with each other are legitimate. The main object of CHAP is to ensure that a user's computer has authorisation to access resources from another computer providing a service.

CHAP can be described as a system that authenticates a user's computer using a technique known as "challenge response". CHAP generates a key transmitted to the user for encrypting the user's password. Passwords stored in the Server table do not have to be encrypted. The main end systems involved in this challenge are CHAP server and a user's computer. Responses to the Server's challenge are without human involvement. It uses a technique known as session management. This means that a request made by a user's computer to gain access to resources of the other end system has to be authenticated when the request is being made. This duration is what is known as a session.

Phases in CHAP challenge and reply processes are as follows:

1. The node or an end system asks the authenticating server if it can use CHAP.
2. The authenticating server replies, telling the end system that it can use CHAP.
3. The authenticating server sends a challenge message to the end system.
4. The node replies with a value that has been calculated with a hash function.
5. The authenticating node receives the reply and checks it against its own calculation of the expected hash value.
6. The authentication sends a new challenge to the node in a sparing manner throughout the entire network.
7. The receiving node or end system should then respond to the challenge.

Masquerading, spoofing in the form of file transfer attack to CHAP server file as well as traffic analysis could be used by attackers and crackers to breach the authentication system and process.

- **Kerberos Authentication Process**

Kerberos authentication process was designed at the Massachusetts Institute of Technology (MIT). This section outlines the steps involved in Kerberos authentication and analysis of key assumptions upon which the authentication system operates.

- **How does Kerberos Work?**

Kerberos uses a ticket granting system for authenticating processes. The system consists of an authentication server, main server and user's computer. A user's request is assigned a ticket. A user also known as a client sends a message containing a password and user id to an authentication server. The authentication server verifies both the password and user's access rights correctness on the main server. If the verification process is successful, the main server releases a ticket to the authentication server. This ticket is encrypted. It consists of user's identification, network address of user's computer and main server's identification. The authentication server sends a ticket back to user's computer. The user's computer requests access to main server using the ticket. The main server decrypts ticket and verifies whether user's identification matches with the plaintext in the message. If it does access is granted.

Assumptions

- Denial of service attacks are not built into the system therefore are not prevented.

Denial of service is a direct attack on the services of network. This is when an attacker prevents the services of a network reaching its customers or clients. It can be very costly. It is not every security system that could prevent denial of service, as a result using Kerberos authentication is equally subject to danger. This assumption also suggests that there should be some level of personal responsibility in ensuring security of any authentication process during Online Business activities.

- Password guessing is handled by the system.

One of the main problems regarding password systems implemented by Online Businesses and banks is that these systems use straight jacket authentication with poor elements of profiling. Straight jacket authentication is an authentication process which is mainly designed to verify a user based on personal details stored by the verifier. This provides attacking avenues for crackers. One of the main techniques employed by these people is profiling. The integrity of a Kerberos authentication can be compromised if a victim is profiled.

- Passwords must be kept secret.

How secret are passwords? Password systems supporting Online Business Systems can be compromised as a result of human vulnerabilities. Kerberos authentication process and other authentication processes should enforce a policy of password management system that reminds users of Online Business Systems to periodically make changes to passwords.

- It assumes that all network devices physically connected to the network are secured.

One would have thought that a better way of providing security for a system is to start from the assumption that network devices connected to a network are not secured. This could help authentication systems such as Kerberos to effectively manage intrusion detection. Intrusions could be detected at access points of network devices that are not well secured.

- Internal clocks used for authentication must be loosely synchronized.

Synchronisation of internal clocks is a process where computer clocks in a local area network or sub-net are harmonised such that they fall in line with other external clocks globally. This enables authentication to take place successfully without discrepancies in global timing. Poor synchronization can serve as a loop hole for an attack.

Authentication and Global Online Business

Successful authentication of a transaction from platforms and networks with poor standards can not be guaranteed. The mindsets of certification bodies and authorities show that the underlying design concept for designing a certificate is usually based on how systems are perceived in advanced economies. Regardless of this, most businesses and standard organisations expect businesses with poor standards to trust the certificates issued to them. This usually occurs due to the trading policies adopted by leading IT companies in advanced economies. Online Business will be more effective and secured if advanced economies strongly engage IT companies in developing economies during development of certificates meant for the global market. The lack of joint system of development explains why EU and other advanced economies legislative framework prohibit persons and businesses from engaging poor nations in electronic business. The lack of engagement and absence of consortium of businesses signed up to any form of trust or certification as a means of authenticating global business transactions among developing economies form part of the reasons why businesses in advanced economies take a stand for discouraging business between advanced and developing economies.

- **Public Key Infrastructure (PKI)**

A public key infrastructure (PKI) combines software, encryption technologies and services that enable corporations and enterprises to protect communication infrastructure, business forecasting and the internet. PKI uses a holistic approach by integrating digital certificates, public key cryptograph, certification, enterprise wide area network architecture. This is cherished from a theoretical point of view. There are however problems associated with certification authorities and bodies, which sometimes cause the conceptual foundations of PKI to shake. There are issues related to trust, law and inconsistencies with existing regulatory frameworks. There is the need for a comprehensive assessment of the role of certification, design and issuing methods among enterprises.

There are different types and common certification schemes available and commonly used for online business security. There is a synergy between certification, standards and the third parties that issue these certificates in the context of business and real world. Although in practice certificates are used thoroughly, problems which are usually associated with them are not explored and resolved satisfactorily. This is because there are numerous trust issues related to this process. There is therefore the need to assess possible solutions viable in resolving these issues in a more holistic manner.

- **Biometric System**

A biometric system is a system that uses measurements of physical attributes to authenticate consumers and customers Williams (2003). Duffy G (2004) states that principle underlying biometric suggest a form of authentication based on who you are rather than something you know. The attributes are usually captured from fingerprints, facial geometry, Iris pattern, Retina, Hand and finger geometry, vein structure, Retina, the structure of the ear, Voice, DNA, Odour etc. The attributes are captured by computer program. The program creates a template for storage in a database. The database could be integrated with an immigration control system, smart card for access control to systems and buildings. In order to authenticate a person, a life scan of the information describing the physical attributes captured have to be matched to the attributes stored in the computer database. The system derives a score which matches the criterion specified for identification and authentication. An audit trail is occasionally generated as an exceptional control measure to check the reliability of the system. Another method of implementing a biometric system is to generate biometric key. This implementation involves a signal component of a physical measurement separated from the noise that comes along the capturing of such data; process the signal resulting in an exact number (key). This should be based on factors such as ambiguity resolution, error correction and noise reduction. Although this method improves security and privacy as a result of the crypto-transformation it is not widely adopted and used in the commercial environment.

Zhang and Yu (2003) discuss the role of biometrics and its applications. Although there is reasonable evidence to suggest that biometric is growing in popularity, there is also scepticism with regards to its effectiveness within industry and the research community. It is asserted in some part of the literature that biometrics relates to the both the study of physiological and behavioural characteristics of a person. The view taken in this book is that it is more appropriate and effective when considered strictly by examining only the physical characteristics of a person. Although some authors assert that biometrics provide the most secure systems, it is an assertion highly debatable, due to the scepticism associated with its accuracy. Physical characteristics such as finger-scan, hand scan, hand geometry, retina scan, iris scan, facial scan, facial geometry, signature scan, dynamic signature verification, voice scan, or speaker verification are usually captured and verified. Biometric technology could be applied in areas such as physical access to buildings (physical access control) as mentioned earlier on. It can also be a useful tool for authenticating e-learning systems. For instance, finger printing is seen as a means of improving online banking transactions and fraud protection. It is also perceived as a method that boosts confidence amongst customers. Scanning technology also need adequate lighting to improve the data set required to be stored in a database for drawing probabilities required for estimating accuracy.

There are challenges associated with using or adopting such a technology. Some of the problems relates to cost and ethics. There are issues also relating to adaptability. Moving such a technology to new environments is not a straight forward task, especially if it is for electronic commerce purposes. There are very high risks associated with the storage of biometric information on a distributed computer network.

- **Smart Card Applications**

A smart card uses an electronic chip to store details about a person, a set of processes or set of authorisation and authentication keys. The information could be stored in infrared format.

Kou, Poon and Knorr (2003) present smart card applications. The makeup and architectural constitution of smart cards and its genesis according to the authors was in 1974. Architecture and the operating systems supporting smart card technology are not as robust of the operating systems supporting desktops. There is a connection between TCP/IP reference model and smart card readers. Examples of some smart cards are the Java and Octopus smart cards. The introduction and application of Octopus smart card in the transport system in Hong Kong almost 12 years ago seem to have had some bearing on the Oyster transport card introduced a few years for Londoners. These cards serve as useful sources of information for homeland security, control and monitoring of road and rail transport systems.

- **Firewalls (Source Lecture Notes in Security Management)**

A fire wall is a software or hardware that filters packets that travels across a network Williams (2004). A packet is the name given to information sent across computer networks. Firewalls therefore allow and disallow non authorised packets across networks. Firewalls are generally classified as restrictive based or connective oriented. In some literature they are also referred to us permissive or service oriented. In general firewalls are meant to implement some aspects of an organisation's information security policy.

There are different ways to configure a firewall. These include but not limited to the following list;

- Screening router
- Dual-Homed Host
- Bastion Host
- Two Routers, One Firewall
- Demilitarized zone (DMZ) Screened Subnet
- Reverse Firewalls
- Tailored firewall

Holden G, (2004), Williams G (2004)

Firewalls and their Configuration

Screening Router

A router that is located between the user or customer's computer and an external computer network, such as the Internet, Intranet and Extranet

Dual-Homed Host

This is usually employed by users of PCs connected to an external computer network, such as the Internet. It supports computers that have a two phase network interface card (NIC). The interface cards assigned to both internal and external computer networks.

Bastioned Host

This is also known as screened host. The Transport Control Protocol (TCP) and User Datagram Protocol (UDP) are made not to function. In other words they are disabled as part of the configuration setup. Most setups make provision for a logged based file designed to keep track of all activities and information traffic on the network.

Two Routers and One Firewall

This is usually deployed in information sensitive environment, such as defence ministries of Government Institutions. A router is located outside to perform an initial packet filtering. The two routers designed as part of the firewall could be used to redirect traffic to subnets within a large organisation.

DMZ Screened Subnet

A unique network that sits at the fence of the internal computer network for managing the filtering of packets in conjunction with a firewall. It supports online web services and other internet based services.

Reverse Firewalls

The setup is designed to manage out going information or packets. Help prevent attacks such as denial of service (DOS), SYN flooding and espionage.

Tailored Firewalls

It is designed to protect specific types of network communication, for example email, SMS and web services.

4.6   Summary

Chapter 4 examined Online Business Security Technologies. There was an overview of standards and protocols that governed security technologies. Protocols, Standards and technologies such as SET, SSL and IPSEC were evaluated. The chapter explained the role of VPN in business to business transactions. There was also an overview of crypto-systems and explanation of their role in security. New trends in authentication were introduced, whiles common models such as PPP, CHAP and Kerberos were also re-examined. There is a discussion on problems associated with authentication. In order for authentication to be successful, key questions such as; are we dealing with the right customer? Does the debit/credit card belong to this person? should be satisfactorily answered. The role of browsers in authentication also formed part of the discussions in this chapter. There is mention of Biometric systems and (PKI) Public Key Infrastructure. Descriptions of firewalls centred on types of firewalls and configuration setups.

Chapter 5

Risk Access Spots (RAS) Common
to Communication Networks

5.1 Introduction

This chapter discusses risk access spots and vulnerability areas common to communication networks. The risk access spots highlighted are primarily based on empirical studies conducted by Williams (2004) among ISPs and network users in Asia, Africa, Europe and North America. The details of the findings could be referenced from Williams (2004). Transmission media, Service Access Points, Electromagnetic Spectrum, Internet Service Providers (ISPs), IP addresses, Ports, Port numbers, MAC address, Computer or Device Server, Cyphertext and Human vulnerabilities due to poor skill set and know-how were among risk access spots identified in the study. The author explains why these elements should be strongly considered as RAS on communication networks. The author believes these areas should be top on the list when carrying out security risk assessment on Online Business systems.

5.2 Risk Access Spots (RAS)

The main RAS examined in this chapter are Transmission Media, Service Access Points, Electromagnetic Spectrum, IP addresses, Ports, Port numbers, MAC address, Computer or Device Server, Cyphertext and Human vulnerabilities.

5.2.1 Transmission Media

The main RAS identified from Transmission media are (SAP) Service Access Points or Connectors, Terminators, (PBX) Private Branch Exchanges, (PABX) Public Automatic Branch Exchanges, the Electromagnetic spectrum comprising Frequency, Wavelength, Amplitude, Baud rate, Base band and Noise and Wired media (twisted pair, coaxial cable, fibre optic etc).

5.2.1.1 (SAP) Service Access Point

SAP is a point of interconnection where two or more (n) number of services exchange information on a computer network in the form of packets[1], digital or analogue signals. This information could be passed from a switch, connector or port of a (LAN) local area network to a (WAN) wide area network via a router. The poor termination of these ports and connectors could result in RAS. Services are enabled by protocols[2], which are either connection, or connectionless oriented. Examples of such protocols are (TCP) Transmission Control Protocol and (UDP) User Datagram Protocol. Services could also be passed through an electromagnetic spectrum. Although most authors do not classify electromagnetic spectrum as a SAP, the author believes that since services could be provided using wireless media, it will be appropriate to consider that as a SAP. A similar notion has been introduced by Deutsche Telecom known as *"Hotspots"*[3]. The application of security threats such as traffic analysis, brute force and sniffing of packet addresses make SAP to become RAS. Techniques such as traffic analysis and packet sniffing could jeopardise the confidentiality of information across the network. The proliferation of wireless networks has created more vulnerability across network layers. This has been as a result of several reasons, including but not limited to the following: Wireless network adapting to the TCP/IP reference model. Problems associated with encrypting the channels of communication on the electromagnetic spectrum, mobile devices adopting different security standards for securing wireless communication and the existence of rogue access points Williams (2004). There are also vulnerabilities associated with wired transmission media. This ranges from twisted pair, coaxial cables and fibre optics as well as submarine cables.

---

[1] Electronic block of data that shows it source and destination via an address
[2] Set of guidelines that govern the format of communication
[3] Access Points within wireless Networks

5.2.1.2 Wireless (ES) Electromagnetic Spectrum

Although there are several definitions given to the electromagnetic spectrum (see Dean 2003), this work defines it as a vacuum or empty space where light or sound waves travel. Electromagnetic spectrum comprises waves. A wave is a form of signal that propagates itself via electrons which are electrically charged as a result of hydraulic pressure, heat or solar energy. In order for the reader to grasp the full meaning of EMS, this section will describe a number of concepts that define the EMS. Concepts such as bandwidth, wavelength, frequency, amplitude and noise within the electromagnetic spectrum are highlighted as risk access spots.

Table 3 – Light waves in the Electromagnetic Spectrum

Signal Radiation	Frequency	Wavelength
Gamma-Rays	$<3 \times 10^{20}$	<1 fm
X-rays	$3 \times 10^{17} - 3 \times 10^{20}$	1 fm – 1nm
Ultra-violet	$7.5 \times 10^{14} - 3 \times 10^{17}$	1nm – 400nm
Visible	$4 \times 10^{14} - 3 \times 10^{14}$	$0.4\mu m - 0.75$
Near-Infra-red	$7.5 \times 10^{13} - 10^{14}$	$0.75\mu m - \mu 3.0\mu m$
Infrared	$2 \times 10^{13} - 10^{14}$	$3.0\mu m - 15 \mu m$
Microwave & Radio waves	$<3 \times 10^{11}$	$>1mn$

5.2.1.2.1 Bandwidth

The bandwidth of a transmission refers to the range of frequencies assigned for communication within the electromagnetic spectrum (EMS). The volume of signals transmitted through the EMS is dependent on the allocation space of the bandwidth. Since the bandwidth is not protected with firewalls or other security mechanisms, it is exposed to intrusion and interference from other signals. Unknown, foreign or illegal signals could be transmitted deliberately or accidentally through these allocated bandwidths. Techniques and methods such as signal propagation using transistors to could reduce or amplify messages within these frequencies. This might result in noise or attenuation[4]. These are access spots and points within the wireless spectrum that is susceptible to attack.

---

[4] The reduction of the power or intensity of a transmitted signal

5.2.1.2.2 Frequency

Frequency refers to the number of transmission cycles in a wave. The nature of frequencies could vary depending of the intensity of the signal transmitted. For instance the human voice could generate a frequency range different from sound emissions from the horn of a train.

5.2.1.2.3 Amplitude

Amplitude refers to the highest point a signal could travel or propagate itself from source to destination of transmission.

5.2.2   Service Provider

A service provider is a trusted third party who ensures the confidentiality, integrity and availability of the information of a service user, also known as a customer. ISPs located across the globe do not employ the same standards. This in itself becomes an avenue where crackers and hackers could exploit. Emphasis has been placed on the management of IP addresses, PORT numbers and MAC addresses.

5.2.2.1 IP Address

IP (Internet Protocol) address comprises a network number and PC or host number allocated internally or externally. The internal allocation of IP address is known as a private unofficial IP address. This consists of a network and a host number. Officially, network numbers are allocated by a non-profit making organisation known as *(ICANN) Internet Corporation for Assigned Names and Numbers.* The rationale behind such a de facto standard is to avoid confusion on the Internet. IP addresses represent the source and destination of packet information. The object of an IP address is primarily to enable routing of information across the Internet. Every network linked or interfaced to the Internet via a router has an IP address. In other words a router has IP information regarding all networks linked to itself.

IP address consists of 32 bits organised in four octets[5]. These bits are converted or translated to decimal numbers that could be read by non-technical persons. For instance an IP address in the form 11000000.10010001.00000001.00000001 could be converted to decimal as 192.145.1.1. An IP address in a decimal form 177.132.1.1 is also represented in binary as 10110001.10000101.00000001.00000001. This is achieved by converting base 10 numbers to base 2 and vice versa. Adopting masquerading techniques could be a means of creating deception among IP addresses. Although standard security systems mask IP addresses, the masks could sometimes be unveiled using virus attacks or brute force. Poor masking of IP addresses could result in RAS. IP numbers stored on routing tables of a router could be a valuable source of information to hackers and intruders Williams (2003). IP's are more associated with routing. There are also routing protocols such as BGP (Border Gateway Protocol) for advertising information on an internet. RIP (Routing Information Protocol), the first type of protocol for routing packets (information). OSPF for overhead information processing functions and IGRP that enable routers to learn more about IP based networks. The IP number could be stored manually or automatically through a learning process. This however depends whether the router or IP device is static or dynamic. IP numbers could be spoofed, and used as a means of congesting communication channels.

5.2.2.2 Sample IP or Routing Table

The transfer or channelling of data from a computer host to another host is known as routing. This process usually comprises three aspects or elements that must be considered on the internet. These are physical address identification, selections of gateways on the internet and symbolic & numeric addressing. The process of identifying gateways and appropriate ports on a network is also known as routing. For example, if a computer wishes to transmit an IP datagram, it must locate the physical address of the destination computer. This can be achieved by implementing a table that could map the IP addresses to physical addresses. The table is usually configured and stored in a file that could be transferred to memory during runtime as part of the start up of the machine, usually known as booting. Communication networks employ a protocol known as ARP (Address Resolution Protocol) defined in RFC (Request for Comments) 826.

---

[5] Block of eight bits

It operates dynamically in the management of the translation table known as ARP cache. The address resolution protocol of UNIX systems could be displayed using the command "arp – a". It is important to note that a computer usually tracks its own physical address during booting by examining hardware and IP address. It reads a configuration or setup file at the boot up time. This is accomplished by the computer an address resolution request in the form of a broadcast when a computer encounters an IP address that cannot map itself to a physical address in cache memory. The general format of an ARP request on an Ethernet is usually represented as follows:

Table 4 – Attributes of Address Resolution Protocol of a life UNIX System

General	Use	Size in Bytes	Typical Values

5.2.2.3 Internet Routing Tables

The main service station of a computer network usually known as the host has a routing table. The host uses the router table to determine which physical interface address to use for outgoing IP datagram. ARP is consulted after initial contact with the routing table in order to determine the physical address. Anytime a computer receives an IP datagram at the interconnection points of a communication network, there are probable occurrences. The datagram is sent to an application that requested it for processing or to another interconnecting point on that network or another network. The UNIX command "netstat – nr" for example displays the state of the routing table. Any hacker or intruder with mediocre knowledge of UNIX shell programming could remotely access this information. This is a vulnerability which most network security systems might not be able to provide a countermeasure. This is because it involves human elements in attack and defence strategies. Below is a snapshot of a router table as displayed on a host at the University of East London in Figure 10.

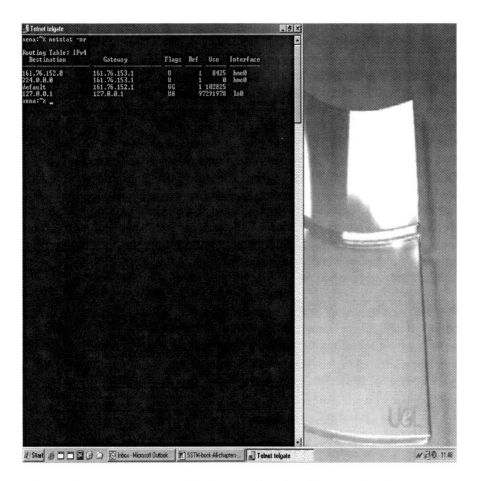

Figure 10 – Router Table from a University of East London host

The router table comprise the following items: Destination of the IP address, the gateway IP address. It is the same as the destination IP address for directly connected destinations. There are flags such as U,G,H and D,M,U that represents a route which is up and running. G means the route is via a gateway. H means the destination address is a host address as different from a network address. Physical Interface identification destination may appear as default. The operations of host machines are directed at the location of destination address in the routing table. If it is not located, it then looks for the destination network address in the routing table, which not found it uses one default address. It is essential to note that a host dedicated to supporting a gateway service located in between several dispersed networks is known as a router. Such a router will usually have a large set of representation in the router table, sometimes more than 64MB. It could run special protocols to interchange routing with other host and routers located across different networks.

5.2.2.4 Ports and Port numbers

A port is a point of connection attached to an electronic device. It might not necessarily be a computer. It could however form an integral part of a computer system. This could range from printers, scanners, cameras, hubs, switches, Network Interface Cards (NICs) and mobile phones. It is usually represented as a 16-bit number between 1 and 65535 used mostly by transport protocols such as TCP and UDP, at the transport layer of TCP/IP and OSI reference models. They are sometimes employed for providing application services. Trojans and sniffing software for scanning port numbers could be used to listen or analyse PORT numbers. Methods of dealing with, and assessing the state of ports vary. Intrusion detection systems or utility managers could be used to examine the state of ports on a network. More sophisticated methods using intelligent agents could also be adopted. It is not the subject of this book to discuss such methods. Figure 2 lists common default Port numbers active on most networks including the Internet.

The port numbers in table five serve as entry points for intruders and hackers if not effectively managed. Port numbers adopted by Trojans could be used in eavesdropping information transmitted via ports that could serve as a means of violating security. A port number selected randomly between 1024 and 65535 will work as long as the number is not in use.

5.2.2.5 Trojans and Port Numbers

A Trojan is a harmful program which infects a computer system when a specific event is triggered. A Trojan usually masquerades itself by hiding its identity. A Trojan derives its name from the Greek Mythology. According to the myth the Greeks tricked the Trojans to carry the horse beyond the security gates and then launched an attack. A Trojan explores a risk access spot by engaging the services of another process on a computer network or system. Table 5 outlines port numbers adopted by Trojans for exploiting vulnerabilities of processes running by users.

Table 5 – Trojans and Port Number

TROJAN	PORT NUMBER
Devil	65000
Deep Throat	UDP 2140 and 3150
Girl Friend	TCP 21544
Evil FTP	23456
Gate Crasher	6969
Remote Grab	7000
Temptation	53001
Angel	4590
Mirage	7789

Source: Dayspring Ltd and NOBA research.

Intrusion detection systems or utility managers could be used to examine the state of ports on a network. More sophisticated methods using intelligent agents could also be adopted. It is not the subject of this book to discuss such methods. Table 6 lists common default, assigned and registered Port numbers active on most networks including the Internet. The services provided the port numbers could serve as vulnerability spots A cracker or hacker could combined an IP address and a Port number to gain access to a service if it is not adequately secured.

Table 6 – Default, Assigned and Registered Port Number

Port Number	Description
80	Web server Port (IP address)
110	Pop server Port (mail services)
25	SMTP Server (works in conjunction with Port 80) mail services
23	Telnet Server
443	Secure Socket Layer server Port
21	FTP Server
1352	Lotus notes RPC Port
1393	Network Log Server
80/tcp/udp	World Wide Web HTTP
118/tcp/udp	SQL Services/Server
109	POP2 (Post Office Protocol) – Version 2
137	NETBIOS Name Service
138	NETBIOS Datagram Service
139	NETBIOS Session Service
143	Internet Message Access Protocol
179	Border Gateway Protocol
197	Directory Location Service
443	HTTP Protocol over
88	Kerberos
79	Finger
66	Oracle SQL.Net
63	Whois++

Source: Dayspring Ltd & NOBA Research

5.2.2.6 MAC Address

MAC is referred to as *Medium Access Control*. The purpose of MAC is basically to identify every physical device or node on a computer network and establish communication amongst these devices or nodes. The physical device in this context refers to the (NIC) Network Interface Card. The address given to the NIC is the MAC address. A typical MAC address will be for instance 0000C0FBB1A4 or 0000C0F958A3. They are referred to in certain literature as LAN, NODE, Adapter, Ethernet or Physical addresses. It is however referred to in this text as MAC address for the sake of consistency. MAC addresses serve as a tool in gaining unauthorised access unto networks. Any information that helps to identify and locate Network Interface Cards such as a MAC address could be detrimental to the security of networks.

Flaws in MAC Address Filtering

A MAC address although meant to be unique could be modified. This flexibility makes the integrity check on a MAC address almost a hopeless one. There are software tools today that enable the alteration of a MAC address, an example of such a tool is "a-MAC address change". This is a source of vulnerability since the MAC address of a computer is designed to create uniqueness for that computer. In the paper "Your 802.11 wireless Network has no clothes" Arbaugh et al (2001), such vulnerabilities were highlighted on a wireless LAN. Organisations deploy wireless network using 802.11 standards. Regrettably 802.11 provide inadequate support for one of the key goals in security management, thus confidentiality. Security goals such as integrity and availability are also not satisfactorily met. These are vulnerabilities beyond physical perimeter control of any organisation.

One of the problems associated with MAC address on wireless platform, is that the address details is broadcast in the open during key management and access control. This enables sniffing of the details, although WEP or any other encryption and authentication mechanism could be enabled at the time of the attack. The sniffing process could be seen as a form of eavesdropping, which is subsequently employed to launch a spoofing attack. So it is not only IP addresses that could be spoofed. MAC addresses can also be spoofed in a similar manner. Figure 11 is an example of how the a-MAC address change software could make such changes. The window shows IP and MAC address details of my personal computer at the University of East London.

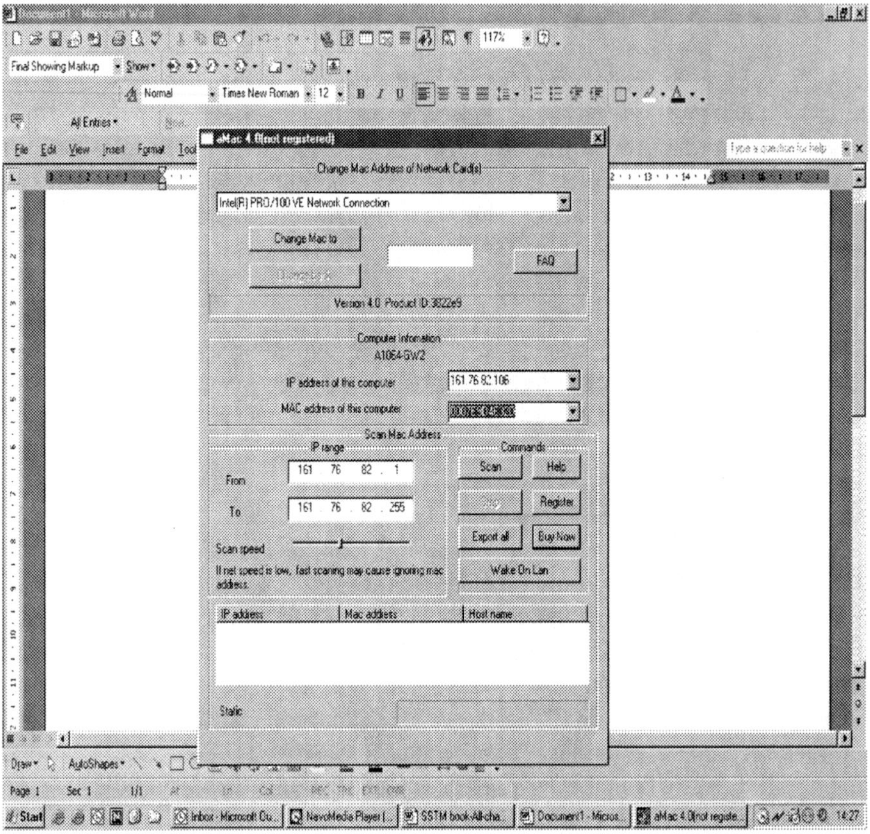

Figure 11 – MAC Address modification

5.2.2.7 Server

A Server is a software resident on a computer or n-computers that respond to a request made by a user via another program known as a *Client* on any electronic network or a computer network. Several connotations and definitions given to a Server refer to it as a computer that replies to request made by users. The author believes that such a definition restricts the application of Servers. The argument put forward here is based on the notion that Servers that respond to Client requests might not necessarily reside on computers. Any electronic device capable of responding to request from Clients regardless of geographical location might be classified as a Server as a matter of principle. Similarly computer programs making request for services on Servers might not be also made from a computer. The deployment device or hardware and the program that responds to such services as defined earlier could also be represented as a Server. The entry point of a Server is via the port number allocated to the Server The Client should also know the port number allocated to the Server in order to gain entry to the Server.

Intruders and hackers could use remote invocations and method calls to access the resources placed on a Server. IP address and Port number could be combined to form a Socket. A Socket derives its address from an IP address and a Port number.

5.2.2.7.1 Server Configuration

The attack on web servers is not alien within the security community. A malware such as "Forbot" successfully spread itself across several networks globally taking advantage of the risk access spot from poor configuration of MySQL servers. This malware infected systems anytime it was remotely stimulated by the attacker. Forbot attacked through the route of the root account of the configuration setup. Refer to appendix 1 for a simulated analysis of the attack. The next paragraph assesses Apache and Tomcat web servers considered to have a high user participation community in industry.

5.2.2.7.2 Apache Server

Apache Server RAS (Risk Access Spot) is well documented in CA-2002-17. This could be exploited by an attacker for launching remote attacks. This RAS is linked to the process which Apache employs to handle encoded data in chunks. For instance the risk access spot is present in versions 1.2.2 and above. The effect of such risk spot or vulnerability is highly dependent on version management discipline adopted and operating system deployed in the application environment or organisation. There are a number of reasons why this form of attack is possible. One of such reasons is the fact that Apache retains facilities for chunk-encoded HTTP request that is likely to permit remote attackers to execute arbitrary code. This view is also shared by the Apache Software foundation an interest group organisation and promoting the use and management of Apache Server. The vulnerability and risk spot was originally published in June 17 2002 in the CVE (Common Vulnerability and Exposures) document by Mitre Corporation. The risk spot in the program could be triggered remotely using illogical request from clients. This is likely to cause a DDOS (distributed denial of service attack).

Apache Web Server provides distributed services in the form of processes consistent with parent and child process management in distributed systems. This makes more than one process available for an attacker. The number of child processes running on the system is likely to correlate with the success factor of an attack. In other words it is linearly related. This conclusion is drawn from the chances an attacker has as a result of number of child processes on the system at the time of the attack. This line of reasoning is popular among researchers and practitioners due to the fact that Apache Server run on a multi-threaded child process when responding to services on windows and netware platforms. The reader should note that recent versions such as Apache 2.0 attempt to rectify this problem by preventing the attacker from executing a code from a remote location. There is also problems associated with divide overflow due to multi child processes, that could affect security due to performance constraints. This is nothing to be surprised of, since there is always a correlation between security and performance. CVE document CVE-2005-2700 highlighted vulnerability and RAS on the SSL_engine_kernel.c in the mod_ssl relased on SSL (Secure Socket Layer) used in conjunction with the Apache Server. This vulnerability is disclosed when using the "SSL Verify Client optional" facility. The global virtual host configuration does not adequately enforce "SSLVerifyClient request" in the appropriate context. This RAS permits remote attackers to get through access control restrictions. This problem is also compounded when the ACL (Access Control List) is not effectively managed. This might arise if certain internal commands are not disabled. The lack of persistent version management and effective monitoring of system dynamics will continue to expose such servers RAS to attackers.

5.2.2.7.3 Tomcat Servers

Tomcat Servers have a history of vulnerability highlighted in a case study published in a bulletin by the U.S department of Energy and Computer incident Advisory capability. This vulnerability is in particular associated with the deployment of JDK (Java Development Kit 1.3.1 or earlier versions in conjunction with the server. For instance according to their investigation an attacker could access files or gain unauthorised access to unexecuted source codes, using a technique known as XSS (cross-site scripting). An attacker could execute arbitrary script. The study was conducted on HP9000 Servers running on HP-UX platforms versions 11.00, 11.11, 11.20 AND 11.22. The findings showed that it served as a RAS. An intruder could exploit that to access files through the execution of arbitrary web scripts. This bulletin is referred to as document N-060. It is also recorded in the CVE as CAN-2003-0042, CAN-2003-0043, CAN-2003-0004. The security of the server is also dependent on the operating system platform. According to the definitive Tomcat guide co-authored by Ian Darwin and Jason Brittain, there could be security breaches if Tomcat and Apache are deployed on the same distributed platform, because of the different security policies utilized. Open ports could also serve as a RAS discussed in previous sections. Poor management of connecting and controlling ports is also detrimental to security.

5.2.3   Human Vulnerabilities and Profiling

A network is as strong as its weakest link. Human vulnerabilities emerge from the human activity system of a network. This includes; awareness, skill, information culture which relates to the way information is kept and disseminated, errors during data entry or system configuration, poor communication between consumers and service providers before and post installation, as well as integrity and trust issues. Lack of motivation due to poor relations between users and service providers also facilitates vulnerability. There is a low level of importance placed on the role played by users and consumers in securing online systems and networks in general. Vulnerabilities are sometimes caused due to the lack of best practices, standards and government policies. In a more general sense human vulnerabilities could be addressed by critically reviewing information culture among users and consumers of online business systems. This means that service providers and stakeholders in online business should examine how information is assessed, kept and disseminated on networks.

Understanding human vulnerabilities by profiling the user is important because it allows service providers to detect unusual behaviour of users. Building the necessary intelligence to provide information on *geographical locations* of users instantly is an effective method for identifying RAS in specific geographical locations. Patterns and frequency of user and system interaction could be a valuable source of information. Conversely, profiling could be used in analysing and identifying the risk and vulnerability spots on network. This could be exploited by an attacker to violate or breach the vulnerability of the system. Similar techniques have been applied in assessing the vulnerability of the internet using GIS tools Robinson N.E (2005). It could be very effective in monitoring Cyber tribes and hidden identities. Profiling has led the way for new techniques such as phishing, ghosting and shadowing. Among these the commonest is phishing.

5.2.3.1 Phishing

Phishing in lay terms is a form of security attack that employs impersona-
tion, deceit and bait techniques on web sites and the Internet. Its goal is to
draw users to a hoax site, win their trust by believing a false representation
as true. It uses FEAR acronym meaning false evidence appearing real.

5.2.3.2 Cyber Tribes

Arreymbi J and Williams G (2006) define Cyber tribes as people in a virtual community that have attributes such as a common language, similar
belief system, culture, traditions, practices and interest. The purpose of
such a tribe just like any tribe is to communicate, disseminate information
and build relationships. In such an environment people who communicate
don't know each other. The question "who is who?" can not be fully answered. Communication is done in virtual space. There is no assurance of
personal interest protection and safeguards. Tribesmen are by themselves.
Members can converse or relate to total strangers for social or business purposes. Examples of such communities are news groups, electronic chat
rooms, and search engines such as google, subject interest based communities etc. Although there are several challenges and issues arising as a result
of these tribes, the immediate ones are spoofing and spam attacks, malware
trace and theft and sale of critical business information.

5.2.4   Cyphertext and Crypto-System

A Cyphertext is an encrypted message. Techniques such as crypt-analysis
and pattern analysis are the most common methods used in decrypting a
Cyphertext. Although the primary objective of encrypting a message is to
ensure confidentiality, this objective is loosely achieved in most cases. It is
argued here that encryption ensures integrity rather than confidentiality.
The application of techniques such as crypt-analysis could permit eavesdropping. See Smart (2003) for detail information on Cryptography. The
new challenges associated with crypto-systems are mainly with the wireless
spectrum. This is because it is almost impossible to successfully encrypt
packets (information) sent across wired and wireless transmission media.

Most crypto-systems are broken and cracked using powerful machines. Therefore, one could speculate that in order for a crypto-system to be secured the computational requirements for breaking such system should be limited. For instance, it will not be computationally viable to break a crypto-system with key length 2^{128}. This implies that such a system in theory is computationally safe. However, having a high performance machine could make such a system porous, if we assume that machine resources from a computational point are unbounded and available in the public domain. It is therefore important for the user of any crypto-system to be aware of the importance of key length applied in protecting data confidentiality and integrity. In summary, the factors include; machine power, technology and length of the key employed in the encryption process. The crypto-systems highlighted in this section, are considered as computationally and conditionally secure. This means the system is secured in so far as machine resources are limited.

5.2.5   Operating Systems Software RAS

Operating system software is the software that manages computer hardware functions and processes. It serves as the communication interface between the suite of application software and hardware. It primary function is computer process, memory and file management.

The analysis of operating systems vulnerabilities in this section applies to PCs, Wired Networks and Wireless Network Infrastructure. In other words the RAS highlighted is evaluated and discussed in both contexts. Operating systems vulnerabilities could emerge as a result of unexpected or malformed input problems, file directory processing, process/command execution, "canonicalization errors", a term used to describe conformity to prescribed specifications, data processing formats, leaks, multiple operation, configuration and error condition identification management errors. This section assesses these risk spots with regards to worm attacks.

The complexity of an operating system's software could lead to inevitable errors and risk access spots which could be exploited by "malware" such as worms. Security vulnerabilities and risk spots could be associated with system components, utilities, routine libraries or operating system kernel.

What is a Worm?

A worm is a Malware which infects computers using reproduction techniques through wireless and wired transmission networks. It is not self propagating like a virus, however could cause a lot of harm. It normally sent by automatic programs.

There is a considerable level of operating system vulnerability well documented. 21.1% in RedHat Linux (allversions), 22.7% in Windows 2000, and 9.5% in Solaris 2.6. It is important to note, that not all vulnerabilities are platform specific, some of them exist on more than one platform, http://www.atstake.com/research/advisories/2003/a010603-1.txt accessed 2005/01/05, http://xforce.iss.net/static/6824.php accessed 2005/01/05

5.2.5.1 Buffer Overflows

What is Buffer Overflow?

A buffer overflow is the term used to represent the condition occurring when temporal memory allocated for a running program, also known as a buffer is not able to cope with data being sent to that memory from other programs. This causes the program to send data to other buffers causing it to overwrite valid data in those buffers.

Buffer overflow sometimes results to risk access spots. In 2003 there were 75% risk spots related to buffer overflows. Worms such as Code Red, Lion, the first known Morris worm and many others took advantage of these spots. The attacker injected worm code to victim's computer through remote execution. The most common type of exploit usually involves overwriting the return address which is stored on the stack within the buffer. This is transferred through execution control to the code in the buffer, or at the end of the buffer Shaneck M (2003).

Network and Internet users experienced a surge of attacks on their host computers including Sasser worm in year 2004. This infected hosts exploiting buffer overflow vulnerability in operating system Local Security, Authority Subsystem Service (LSASS). The default system permits services to be accessible remotely in Windows operating systems. The exploit was carried out by sending specially crafted packet to Local Security Authority Directory Service interface "DsRolepDebugDumpRoutine()" logging function. The function is used to write logging information to a file DCPROMO.LOG. Input string arguments for the function are passed to 2kb stack buffer without any bounds checking. Sasser overwrites return address of the stack that points to its shell code Ferrie, Perriot (2004). In August 2003, the Blaster worm also attacked vulnerable operating systems. It exploited operating system vulnerability on RPC and DCOM interface on a remote system. This was possible because RPC stub does not apply a thorough data input process under certain conditions. Hence, Blaster worm was able to send specially formed package that caused buffer overflow in the DCOM service. The vulnerability occurs in HRESULT CoGetInstanceFromFile() function, where sixth parameter, a NetBIOS server name, is passed without bounds checking. It has a 32-byte buffer on the stack set. Thus, Blaster overwrites the address and execution is returned to worm code eEye (2003).

5.2.5.2 Format String and Denial of Service attack

There are vulnerabilities related to Format string as a result of user inputs. It is possible to read and write or cause denial of service attacks Newsham (2003). For example, format string vulnerability in Mac OS X point to point protocol daemon (pppd). It is possible to read arbitrary data out of pppd's process http://www.atstake.com/research/advisories/2004/a022304-1.txt accessed 2005/01/01

5.2.5.3 Syntax Grammar Violation and Denial of Service Attack

This risk spot occur when input data to a function is missing an argument, when there is wrong data type. For instance, Red Hat Linux default print job manager Internet Printing Protocol, can process one service at a time. This enables a remote attacker to make partial request that does not time out. This causes denial of service attack http://www.redhat.com/support/errata/RHSA-2003171.html accessed 2004/12/01

5.2.5.4 Character Mismanagement

There are characters in programs, which are treated as special or control characters, for example end of input delimiter "." in mail message data. Internal routine in Samba Web administration tool in Red Hat causes buffer overflow. This makes it possible for a remote attacker to execute arbitrary code. The risk spot emerges when the routine is not able to handle invalid character in decoding base 64 data http://www.redhat.com/support/errata/ accessed 2003/12/02.

5.2.5.5 Null Dereference Error

This occurs when pointers have not been checked before manipulating them. Pointers may point data or a null value. Null dereference in Windows Security Software Provider interface that leaves a risk spot likely to allow remote attackers denial of service during authentication protocol selection. Microsoft (2004).

5.2.5.6 File or Directory Processing

Classical directory traversal vulnerability is usually when system allows remote attacker to access files via "./"(current directory) and "../" (parent directory) and many other variations on the machine. "Nimda" worm is partly based on directory traversal vulnerability in internet information services. "TNEF" is a program in Linux which extracts compressed e-mails. The compressed file includes path name, where it should be extracted. The program extracts without verification of the folder in the path. It can cause sensitive files to be overwritten like local password database Bugtraq (2003). This could result in information leak. For example, pages made in PHP, with default configuration allow remote attackers to obtain path for an include file. It is performed via trailing slash in request which produces error message with a path directory Bugtaq (2003).

Windows MS-DOS device names (DDNs) are reserved names by operating system that cannot use naming files or directories. Remote attacker can cause denial of service by specifying pathname that has more than one DDN in its pathname in Windows operating system.

5.2.5.7 Command Execution and Metacharacter

A metacharacter is a character which provides information about other characters including process information. Misuse of metacharacter flaw exists in Kerberos network authentication system's FTP client. When retrieving a file with a filename beginning with a pipe character, the client will pass the filename to the command shell in a system call.

5.2.5.8 Program Argument Modification or Argument Injection

Unexpected input arguments can result in unexpected behaviour of a system. For example, specifying "–froot" option in "rlogin" service handler in Linux operating systems causes immediate switch by sending the user into a root shell. Loophole in Windows Help and Support Centre allows attackers to execute arbitrary code. The program does not properly authenticate with quote symbols in the HCP protocol URLs, therefore, allows remote attacker to inject scripting code into a pre-existing file.

5.2.5.9 Canonicalization Errors

Canonicalisation errors occur when a system makes decision on a name, a folder name, a filename, a Web address, without considering that there can be more than one way to express it. For example, case sensitivity, Task Manager in Windows 2000 does not allow terminate upper case named processes for "winlogon.exe", "csrss.exe", "smss.exe" and "services.exe". This allows an attacker to inject processes, e.g. worms that cannot be stopped CVE (2001).

5.2.5.10 Leaks

It is sometimes possible to gather information from a host, which is not intended to be shared over the Internet. Information can be gathered about host before attack. For example, some open-source firewalls can allow attacker to determine whether a port is filtered or not. In response, the message a remote attacker obtains from that host "time-to-live" value is set different than default one therefore making it adequate to determine the leak. Multiple platform Ethernet Network Interface Card (NIC) device drivers incorrectly handle frame padding that allows attackers to view portions of kernel memory or previously sent packets. By sending message that verifies network layer communications, portions of information are returned in request. Linux kernel does not properly initialise memory in the Linux ext3 file system code. This causes information leak where some old blocks of memory can be read. It contains old data from the system memory.

Memory leak is often triggered by improper handling of malformed data or unexpectedly interrupted sessions. In such cases a program does not release memory that it does not need any more. As a result, it consumes more and more memory that leads to program crash e.g. improper decrement of counter when error occurs in Linux do_fork function CVE (2004). Incomplete resource release arises due to unexpected error. Names within Windows deployed as part of the Remote Procedure Call (RPC) services fail to close properly. This allows attackers to create resource exhaustion via series of connections, containing malformed data.

5.2.5.11 Multiple Operation Errors

This is the inability to handle out-of-order actions, race condition or duplicate operation. For example, double free condition is an attempt made to free a memory area, which has been previously released or freed. Double-free vulnerability in Windows library allows attackers by sending crafted request cause denial of service or even execute arbitrary code CVE (2004).

5.2.5.12 Operating System Configuration Errors

It is important that operating systems must be secure at installation stage. Default vendor values settings must ensure minimum security level, e.g. no non-essential services running, default network accessibility. However, this is only a recent concern. *"In previous Windows versions, almost every bell and whistle was installed and started requiring the system administrator to lock down the device afterward."* Gadue (2004). An example is file permission problem in Red Hat Linux. The installation program writes some files with the wrong world-writeable permissions.

5.2.5.13 Error Condition Identification/Management Error

These are errors that arise in error detection process, e.g. in program handler implementation or logging security-critical events. This apparent lack of password logging exists in HP-UX operating system, when an attacker is allowed to make endless password attempts. Attackers can use brute force to guess passwords CVE (2001).

5.2.5.14 Asymmetric Resource Consumption

This happens when one entity makes another one consume more resources than necessary. For example, multiple TCP implementations on various platforms are vulnerable to denial of service attack. This can be accomplished by requesting for large amounts of data and setting very low value for Maximum Segment Size parameter. Mac OS systems generate large ICMP datagrams in response to malformed datagrams. It can result to network flood. The TCP/IP fragment reassembly in Red Hat Linux and allow attackers to create large CPU consumption via packets that trigger large number of hash table collisions.

5.2.5.15 Insufficient Resource Pool

This occurs when software has no sufficient resources to handle peak demand. This can disable others to access the resource. NetScreen operating system does not support maximum number of concurrent connections. This enables attackers to create resource exhaustion via port scan to external network.

5.2.5.16 Authentication Error

This permits a protected operation to be invoked without proper check of the invoking agent. It can happen when resources are accessed before authentication function is called. Vulnerability can exist if there is an alternative name to authenticate. Partial password comparison error exists in Windows File and Print Sharing service which allows remote attacker to send a 1-byte password, which matches first symbol of real password. This vulnerability was successfully exploited by "W32.Opaserv.Worm". The worm attempts to replicate across open network by guessing the password and copying itself to the remote computer CVE (2000), Symantec (2004).

Default configuration NetBIOS enabled could also expose Windows XP hidden scripts such as "C$, ADMIN$". A good guess could result in a successful attack. This is usually dependent on poor configuration rather than vulnerability of a feature associated with an Operating System.

Businesses are using mobile devices, especially smart phones and PDA's with processing power of PCs for sending emails, fetching information from Corporate Intranet and surfing the Internet for public information relevant to electronic business. The security vulnerabilities and RAS discussed are applicable to operating systems deployed on smart phones. Below is a synopsis of a security review which the author of this book conducted on the blackberry smart phone.

5.2.6   Smart Phone Review

This section presents s synopsis of an independent expert review on wireless blackberry smart phone conducted for Research in Motion Limited and a BT representative in London.

Overview of Blackberry Smart Phone Design Architecture

1. The internal security model of BlackBerry (BB) Enterprise Solution Components comprises the BB Wireless handheld Device (WHHD), Handheld Software, Desktop Software and an Enterprise Server.

2. The peripheral & external security model of BB comprises BB Enterprise Server and Microsoft Exchange Server (MES) leverage.

Comments to Blackberry Representative:

"NB: There is without a doubt comprehensive data encryption between the WHHD and BB Enterprise Server making transit data well protected. Confidentiality does not seem to be an issue. There is however the need to assess issues regarding availability and Integrity with particular reference to Malware, example viruses and worms, since there are new types of Malware that acts as software agents and possess a decent level of Intelligence.

The application of the SRP (Server Routing Protocol) on the TCP/IP suite provides accessibility to entry points between BB Enterprise Server and the Wireless Handheld Device. There are also risk access spots that could be exploited during synchronization of data between WHHD, Desktops, BB enterprise Server, Microsoft Exchange Servers.

There are new attacks employed that enable a user of a network to borrow another user's IP and MAC address on a communication network. This could be used as an attacking method during synchronisation between, BB Exchange Server and MES".

5.2.7   Proposed Ideas to RIM Ltd After Review

"A securtiy model with self induced/swarm Intelligence capability that acts as an agent for managing malware attack as part of the BB Operating System. We are looking at an anti-malware that is self adaptive. This is contrary to traditional anti-malware software that has to be downloaded as different versions on PCs. and mobile devices.

The underlying defence idea is not to eliminate the malware, but rather highly control it's effectiveness and destruction ability and make it impotent, subsequently discarding it via a garbage collector".

5.3   Summary

Chapter 5 examined Risk Access Spots (RAS) common to communication networks. The RAS is chosen based on empirical studies conducted in a study by Williams (2003). Most of the RAS identified are also generally accepted as critical risk or vulnerability spots on communication networks among practitioners and researchers in industry and academia. The RAS identified and evaluated included, Transmission media, cables, Electromagnetic Spectrum (EMS), Service Providers, IP addresses, port and port numbers, computer and network servers, MAC address and the Human activity system. There is review of two common servers, the apache and tomcat servers. The chapter also examines the human activity system with respect to profiling. Phishing and cybertribalism techniques associated with profiling were explained. Crypto systems were revisited in this chapter. There was detail analysis of risks access spots associated with operating system software.

Chapter 6

Methods of Attacks on Risk Access Spots:
Online Information Warfare

6.1 Introduction

This chapter presents a pedagogical view of the methods employed by attackers, hackers, electronic criminals in exploiting vulnerable systems as reviewed and discussed in chapter 5. The methods of attack also include a wide range of common techniques for penetration testing usually adopted to expose risk access spots on electronic and on-line business communication networks. The methods for attack centres on transmission media (Wired and Wireless spectrum, Service Access Points (SAP), Routing Table & IP address, Port and Port number, MAC address, Server, User Profiles, Cyphertext and Crypto-systems and Operating Systems highlighted in previous chapter. The defence and management strategies for handling these attacks on a communication network have been presented in chapters 4, 7, 8 and 9.

The attacks have been classified into **methods** and **software tools**. The methods of attacks cover the following **22 methods**; Brute Force, Masquerading, Traffic Analysis, Profiling, Scavenging, Roaming and Scouting, Spoofing (Web, DNS, IP), Stealth Attacks, Denial of Service (DOS) (SYN Flood, Smurf, TCP ACK Flooding etc), Distributed Denial of Service (DDOS), Malware propagation (Worms, Viruses, Bots, Spyware) Man in the Middle, Replay, TCP Session Hijacking, ARP (Address Resolution Protocol) pollution, IP Fragmentation, Replay, TCP Session Hijacking, Password conjecture and guesswork, Backdoor, Mobile codes and electronic bombs, Ping, Permutation Analysis. Software tools and utility computer programs used by hackers to exploit vulnerabilities are discussed in this chapter.

6.2 Overview of Attacks

This section presents an overview of the methods of attack as outlined in section 6.1. The analysis comprises descriptions, flowchart representation and experiments for the purposes of illustrations.

6.2.1   Attack 1

DOS and DDOS Attack on Ports, Protocols and Applications

Service request of applications are usually made via ports on the host computer of a Service Provider. For example, most web services are provided via port 80. Vulnerability could lie within the program code of the application providing the service. This could be exploited by a remote user attempting to look for a service. This section illustrates the process of launching a DOS or DDOS attack by disrupting the services provided by an application using a port as its communication channel. Buffer overflows could be a risk access spot that could be generated by corrupting the source or executable code of the application. An attacker could dump several lines of code in different syntax or programming language as a way of disrupting the functionality of the application. An application could also be exploited to consume system resources. An attacker could also compel an application to misbehave or malfunction. This is possible although ports are usually closed as a routine measure; applications do not have that form of self defence mechanism. This is common to most applications. A client or user that aims to attack using a DOS attack could sometimes succeed by simply sending several ping messages or request to a server, making it unable to cope eventually.

6.2.2   Attack 2

SYN Flooding

This is a form of attack that is usually launched during TCP client server interaction. A client or user makes a request to a server, for a service such as video streaming or directory search. This is preceded by a TCP handshake in the form of TCP SYN and ACK packet exchange. Below is a flowchart and diagram illustrating this process.

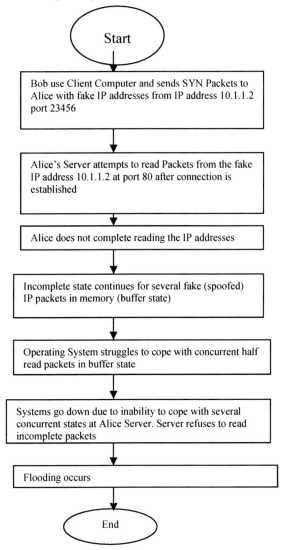

Figure 12 – Flowchart showing the process of interaction of SYN flooding

Description of Figure 12 Simulating SYN Flooding Attack

Figure 12 is a simulated flowchart illustrating how a client machine could launch a denial of service attack via SYN Flooding. In this attack there are two persons involved. They are Bob and Alice. Bob use Client Computer and sends SYN Packets to Alice with fake IP addresses from IP address 10.1.1.2 port 23456. Alice's Server attempts to read Packets from the fake IP address 10.1.1.2 at port 80 after connection is established. Alice "reads" but does not complete the process of reading the IP addresses sent by Bob. The incomplete state continues for several spoofed (fake) IP packets in memory (buffer state). Operating System struggles to cope with concurrent half read packets (data) in buffer state. The system fails and becomes intolerant due to inability to cope with several concurrent states at Alice's Server machine. The server refuses to read incomplete packets. Flooding occurs resulting to a Denial of Service (DOS) attack.

SYN vulnerability is primarily revealed during the establishment of a connection between a client and server using TCP. The SYN and ACK 3 way exchange could be blocked or made unsuccessful when a client's IP address is spoofed, a terminology used to represent a form of deception or counterfeit service request made by a client. This compels the server to be in an indefinite response loop in an attempt to send an ACK to the genuine client that established the handshake with the server. This misdirection indicates a successful spoofing strategy resulting in a DOS attack.

6.2.3 Attack 3

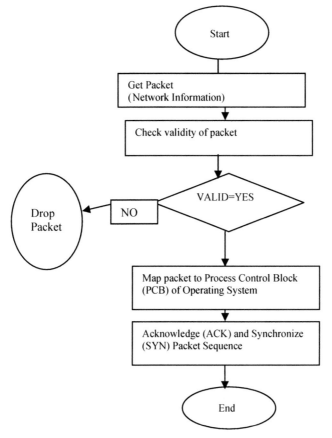

Figure 13 – Flowchart showing the process of interaction of ACK Flooding

Description of Figure 13

The attack starts with a packet sent to a network node through a network or socket address using a "ping" command. The validity of the packet is checked by verifying the IP address. If the packet is valid it is likely to be left through to the network node under attack. This is sent to the process control block (PCB). The PCB is that part of the operating system responsible for scheduling data being processed.

6.2.4   Attack 4 - Scavenger Attack

Scavenger Attack on Hostnames using "Ifconfig" Command:

A hostname is the name allocated to a computer that provides services to other computers. It can also represent a user or client's computer which serves other computers. For example a home computer can serve as a local host when it provides remote services to other computers on a public network such as the internet. It can also be referred to as the computer that serves users usually called the server.

Displaying Hostnames and Network Information from a UNIX Operating System Platform using "Ifconfig" Command:

Ifconfig
- $: Ifconfig – Command views the IP address and other information about hosts's interface to the network.

    - Eg: ifconfig – a

Comments: The above command leads to the results below:

- lo0:   flags=849<UP,   LOOPBACK,   RUNNING, MULTICAST> mtu 8232
inet 127.0.0.1 netmask ff000000
le0: flags=863<UP BROADAST, NOTRALLERS, RUNNING, MLTICAST >mtu 1500
inet 192.102.10.89 netmask ffffff00 broadcast 192.102.10.255

NB: 127:0.0.1 is destination address for (local host), whereas 192.102.10.89 is your host's actual IP address, by which it is known to the outside world

NB: The "Ifconfig" is usually located at/sbin directory on UNIX operating system platform. The "ifconfig" command and utility is used by the systems manager to modify the configuration of a network interface. Network managers usually use that for allocating an address to a network interface during configuration. Given this network information an attacker can use it to change the network interface address from local and remote positions. The command can also be used to manipulate the DHCP (Dynamic Host Configuration Protocol). DHCP is a protocol for automatically assigning IP addresses to network devices. It keeps track of both static and dynamic IP addresses. This means that intervention of its function with "ifconfig" command is likely to destabilize its role of dynamic address allocation. This command can be executed remotely using a script written in Java or Visual Basic.

6.2.5   Attack 5 - Attacking Hosts Database

Displaying domain names and IP addresses of the hosts on your network using "cat/etc/hosts" command.

The "hosts" file is a local database for matching hosts and internet protocol addresses. Another database for holding addresses of domains and resolving names when clients make a request to a host known as DNS (Domain Naming Service) can be combined with the host file by an attacker to launch an attack that can terminated network functions. A host can have many IP addresses. The database of the host has the following format.

| Host | IP-address | Hostname | Alias |

6.2.6   Attack 6 - Using Nslookup

Displaying the IP address of a host whose name is passed as a command line argument to it using "nslookup" command:

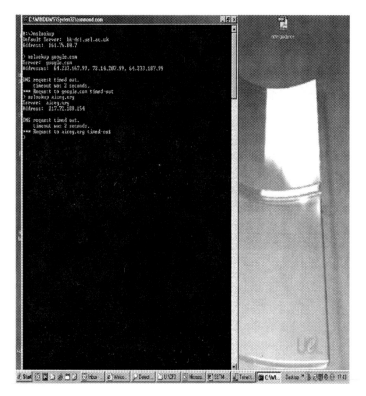

Figure 14 – Nslookup
Source: UEL host

6.2.7   Attack 7 - Using "Finger" Command

"Finger" command displays and captures information about a user's computer on a network. The command can display information about a user on a specified host running the "finger" command. It can also provide information on the user you want information about on the specified computer host or server. Figure 15 is a screen dump of the "finger" command. The command "finger Godfried Williams" has displayed the user ids and details associated with other people with "Williams" as a last on the network. It has also showed the path which stores the user ids.

Telnet Telgate

****

If you are using this machine to access UEL servers from the Internet, please use the new proxy server "UEL gate" or contact the IT dept

Xena: ~% finger Godfried Williams
Login name : godfried   In real life: Godfried Williams
Directory: / home/staff/godfried   Shell: usr/local/bin/tcsh
On since Jul 6 17:55:33 on pts/16 from extrix.uel.ac.uk
No unread mail
No plan.
Login name : wil3201h   In real life: Gray Ronal Williams
Directory: /mnt/home1/1s/hnd90/wil3201h Shell:usr/local/bin/tcsh
Never logged in.
No unread mail
No plan.
Login name : wil1751j   In real life: Karen Williams
Directory: /mnt/home2/soc/ba91/wil1751j Shell:usr/local/bin/tcsh
Never logged in.
No unread mail
No plan.
Login name : wil1343j   In real life: Cleopatra Williams
Directory: /mnt/home2/csu/ba91/wil1343j Shell:usr/local/bin/tcsh
Never logged in.
No unread mail
No plan.
Login name : david16   In real life: David Williams
Directory: /mnt/home2/ee/staff/david16 Shell:usr/local/bin/tcsh
Never logged in.
No unread mail
No plan.

Figure 15 – Finger command
Source: UEL host

6.2.8   Attack 8 - "Ipconfig and Ping" Attack

Attacker can use "Ipconfig and ping" commands to launch a DOS or Spoofing attack.

C:\WINDOWS\ System32\command.com
H:\> ipconfig
Windows IP Configuration
Ethernet Adaptor Local Area Connection:
Connection-specific DNS Suffix.: uel.ac.uk IP Address………………..…..: 161.75.82.106 Subnet Mask………………..…..: 255.255.248.0 IP Address………………..…...: 161.75.80.1
H:\> ping 161.76.82.106
Ping 161.76.82.106 with 32 bytes of data:
Replay from 161.76.82.106: bytes 32 time <1ms TTL=128 Replay from 161.76.82.106: bytes 32 time <1ms TTL=128 Replay from 161.76.82.106: bytes 32 time <1ms TTL=128 Replay from 161.76.82.106: bytes 32 time <1ms TTL=128
Ping statistics for 161.76.82.106: Packets: Sent = 4, Received = 4, Lost = 0 (0% loss), Approximate round trip times in milli-seconds: Minimum = 0ms, Maximum = 0ms, Average = 0ms
H:\>

Figure 16 – Screen dump of ipconfig command
Source: UEL host

Attacks 9 to 13 are Utility Tools Available for Hacking

The utility programs listed below could be used for penetration testing purposes. Consumers and organisations could use any of these tools on their home network to test security of their network infrastructure.

6.2.9   Attack 9 - Cain and Abel

It is a password recovery tool for Microsoft Operating Systems used by network administrators to test their system. It is also exploited by hackers for cracking encrypted passwords using dictionary attacks or crypt-analysis. The application of the tool can render systems vulnerable by taking advantage of weaknesses in protocols, cache memory and authentication granting systems. It has the capability of cracking VoIP conversations, breaking open scrambled passwords as well as tracking the routes of IP packets on a network. On a positive note it can be used for digital investigation or computer forensics. More recent development of the tools enables users to poison router table information.

6.2.10   Attack 10 - John the Ripper

A password cracker effective on UNIX and Windows operating system platform. The following command is based on a dictionary attack using a word list in a password file. The words listed in the dictionary covers a common set of words likely to be used for a password attack. John the Ripper comes with a number of command line options.

Session = name
Stdout =length
Status=name

The above option is sent through a UNIX pipe, which simply handles input output data. JRP comes with a utility for bruteforce attacks, which can crack encrypted passwords with OpenBSD, DES, MD5 and Blowfish. The command below is can detect a password weakness and attend to crack it.

Godfried – wordlist = password.password.

6.2.11 Attack 11 - NMAP

Used for scanning ports of large networks

6.2.12 Attack 12 - Netstumbler

A wireless utility program that detects the presence of WLANs

6.2.13 Attack 13 - Snort

Snort works as a packet analyser and sniffer. A packet sniifer is a program that reads packets of data in transmission on a network. Packets read may include passwords, credit and debit card details. The packets are in the form of plaintext. Remember that there are some password systems which do not encrypt. A packet sniifer can be installed on a network without permission from an administrator.

6.2.14 Attack 14 - Mobile Codes

A mobile code is a code that can suspend execution on one system and migrate onto another to restart the execution. It is also a code that can be executed remotely to a victim's machine.

Design Goal

It is primarily designed to optimise performance of distributed systems and networks. It can however be exploited for malicious gains. Examples of mobile code programming tools are Javascripts and ActiveX.

Architecture of a Mobile Code System

The simplest mobility system model comprises a program code, dynamic states or instances of the code and a code execution platform. The different types of attacks launched by mobile codes take the form of mobile code to mobile platform, mobile platform to mobile code or mobile code to mobile code attacks.

Architecture of Malicious Mobile Code

Example 1 – Malicious message to *Godfried Williams*

```
# Message
<Script> malicious code </script>
#End of message
```

The code can be embedded as a malicious html tag intended for *Godfried Williams*.

Example 2 – Malicious web link

```
# Web link
<A HREF="http://Godfried.com/news.cgi?
news = <script> malicious remote code </script>"> Please click this for
latest channel 1 news </A>
```

This could be launched as Phishing, Trojan or Worm attacks. Clicking this link can trigger remote execution of a code.

6.2.15   Attack 15 - Worm and DOS (Denial of Service)

Worms use remote code execution by targeting buffer spaces in running programs as well as exploring vulnerabilities such as; 1. Format string errors due to human errors 2. Buffer overflows 3. Syntax and grammar violation due to missing arguments or wrong data type violation in system programs 4. Character mismanagement 5. Character mismanagement 6. Poor references to program variables and data types 7. Information gathered from a host on a network not intended to be distributed across the network 8. Multiple operation errors due to poor synchronization and poor handling of deadlocks in computer memory 9 A process that consumes more resource than other processes in memory.

It is also known as "asymmetric" resource consumption 10 Operating system configuration errors. Refer to chapter 5 for details on vulnerabilities.

6.2.16   Attack 16 - Brute Force

Dictionary attack for cracking password on computer systems or networks. It uses an exhaustive key search to crack a Ciphertext by referencing to a comprehensive dictionary. It is however computationally demanding.

6.2.17   Attack 17 - Backdoors

Backdoors are used for gaining remote entry to networks. They are tools used by network administrators. Examples of such tools are Back Orifice, Subseven and Netbus. These tools can allow remote control and management of a computer.

6.2.18   Attack 18

Trojans

6.2.19   Attack 19

Stealth - This attack exploits vulnerabilities on router tables and network information.

6.2.20 Attack 20

Electronic Bombs

6.2.21   Attack 21

Phishing - A social intelligence tool deceiving users in Online Business. It adopts techniques such as profiling and identity theft. This type of attack capitalizes on human vulnerability RAS.

6.2.22 Attack 22

Roaming and foot printing

6.3   Summary

Chapter 6 presented a pedagogical view of methods used by hackers and crackers to exploit risk access spots and network vulnerabilities in Online Business Systems. The attacks exploited on vulnerabilities such as transmission media (Wired and Wireless spectrum, Service Access Points (SAP), Routing Table & IP address, Port and Port number, MAC address, Server, User Profiles, Cyphertext and Crypto-systems and Operating Systems. The defence and management strategies for handling these attacks on a communication network supporting Online Business has been presented in chapters 4, 7, 8 and 9.

The methods of attacks cover methods and tools such as Brute Force, Traffic Analysis using tools such as Snort, Profiling, Scavenging, Roaming and Scouting, Spoofing (Web, DNS, IP), Stealth Attacks, Denial of Service (DOS) (SYN Flood, Smurf, TCP ACK Flooding etc), Distributed Denial of Service (DDOS), Malware propagation (Worms, Viruses, Bots, Spyware), Man in the Middle, Replay, TCP Session Hijacking, ARP (Address Resolution Protocol) pollution, IP Fragmentation, Replay, TCP Session Hijacking, Password conjecture and guesswork, Backdoor, Ping, Permutation analysis and exhaustive key search. Software tools and utility computer programs used by hackers to exploit vulnerabilities were discussed.

Chapter 7

Security Risk Modelling

7.1   Introduction

Security and risk models generally map out security and risk requirements in an information system or the process of developing such a system. It is also used to determine and simulate the behaviour of such systems, as a means of understanding details of changes likely to occur when the system is functioning.

This chapter is an assessment of existing security and risk models and how they compare and contrast with the proposed SSTM model on communication networks. The analysis covers common and widely deployed models such as CRAMM, OCTAVE, ASSET, JAVA SECURITY MODEL and HOLISTIC SECURITY and ISMM.

7.2   Overview of Existing Methods and Approaches

7.2.1   OCTAVE

OCTAVE (Operationally Critically Threat, Asset and Vulnerability Evaluation is a method for evaluating security risk. Its proponents and advocates deem it to be comprehensive, systematic and context driven. In OCTAVE, confidentiality, integrity and availability are evaluated in conjunction with the IT infrastructure of the organisation under investigation. OCTAVE applies a three phase methodology. The phases are; Build Asset Based Threat Profiles, Identify Infrastructure Vulnerabilities and Develop Security Strategy and Plans.

Phase 1: This is an assessment of an organisation's key assets, threats associated with these assets and the security needs of the assets identified. The risk and security management team identifies strategies adopted by the organisation to secure its ICT infrastructure.

Phase 2: Build Asset - Based Threat Profiles - An organisation's ICT Infrastructure is assessed. An audit is performed to identify operational elements of the ICT infrastructure. This is based on the information gathered by compiling notes on existing infrastructure.

Phase 3: Develop Security Strategy and plans - A risk assessment is carried out at this phase. Infrastructure gathered from phase 1 and 2 are analysed to identify risks to the organisation, and subsequently assessed to determine the impact of risk to the organisation's mission or goals. A strategy for protecting and mitigating high level risk are developed.

Pictorial Representation of OCTAVE

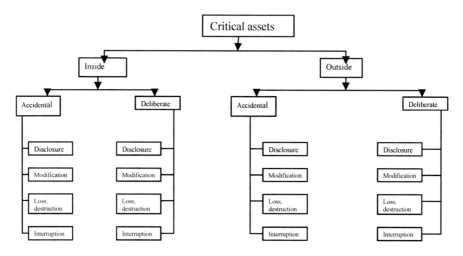

Figure 17 – Human actors using network access

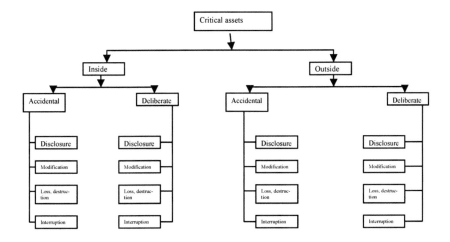

Figure 18 – Human actors using physical access

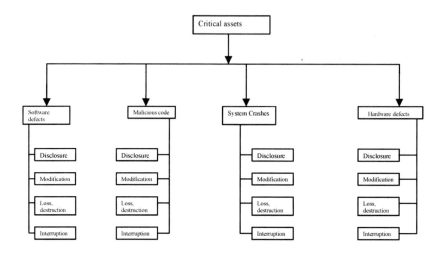

Figure 19 – System Problems

7.2.2   How Does OCTAVE Define Threat?

OCTAVE perceives or defines threat as an indication of a potential undesir-able danger. An example is an attacker initiating a DOS (Denial of Service) attack against an organisation's file server.

Table 7 – Properties of threat in OCTAVE

Property	Description
Asset	Anything with a value in an organisation
Actor	Anything be it a person, an item or a process that can compromise the confidentiality, integrity and availability of an organisation.
Motive	An indication whether the actors actions were deliberate or accidental
Outcome	Effects or results of post confidentiality, integrity and availability violation.

The general threat profiles according to the developers could be customised to meet the needs of different organisations. This can be approached by inserting and deleting threats, which are not applicable to particular organi-sation. Whiles some organisations might apply the standard threat profiles, others may choose to tailor it to their security needs and requirements.

7.2.3   How Do you Create and Use a Threat Profile?

Workshops and seminars are conducted with the particular organisation's employees. This is done to elicit information requirements associated with the threats that could compromise the confidentiality, integrity and availability of that organisation. This information is used to create threat profiles for critical assets of the organisation's systems and information assets.

Different scenarios are built based on the areas of concern highlighted by employees at operational, tactical and strategic levels of the organisation. The main objective of the workshops is to identify important assets, concerns with specific areas and processes, (this could be perceived risk linked to the assets). It is also designed to understand strategies used by the organisation and associated vulnerabilities. At the end of phase 1, areas of concerns are matched to threat properties identified. Areas of concern are mapped unto users using the network access tree highlighted in figure 17. In summary OCTAVE allows security risk evaluation that assist organisations to determine risks associated with confidentiality, integrity and availability of critical information assets. This process is usually engineered by an interdisciplinary team. Potential threats are represented using hierarchical structures.

7.3   Overview of CRAMM

CRAMM is an acronym for United Kingdom's Risk Analysis and Management Method. It applies a structured approach to risk analysis. It is designed to enable reviewers conduct detail security audit on information systems. According to government and practitioners, it is a tool that should be used by experienced or certified practitioners. The concept underlying CRAMM is that risk is dependent on asset values, threats and vulnerabilities. The values of these parameters are evaluated by the practitioner when carrying out risk analysis or management. The risk analysis interview is conducted with owners of the assets, users of the system being analysed, technical support team and the security department where appropriate.

The outcome of CRAMM is usually to depict countermeasures necessary to mitigate risk identified during risk analysis. The need to mainly recruit trained practitioners in using CRAMM can be viewed as a weakness of the tool. This is based on factors such as cost for SMEs, flexibility, adaptation and adoption by other risk analysts who may not be familiar with the tool. Although it is sensible and important that the users of the tool are experienced with the application of CRAMM, it lacks the openness that permits professionals to transfer their skills to the CRAMM environment or organisation.

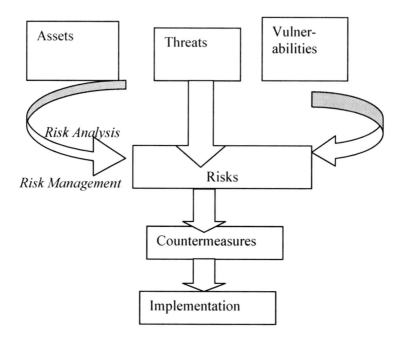

Figure 20 – Conceptual diagram of CRAMM

The key stages in CRAMM are as follows; measure your risk, understand your risk, set a target for your risk, manage your risk, adopt standards.

7.3.1   Key Stages in CRAMM

7.3.1.1 Measuring Your Risk

Determining the scope of this risk and the extent to which it could be quantified is not an easy task. This is because risk is very qualitative as such could effectively be measured indirectly by assessing the cost associated with threat. According to proponents of CRAMM, it has the toolset that enables risk analyst to measure risk. Whether it does that effectively or not is not something that could be solely judged in this book. The view taken with regards to this is simply based on the notion that risk is highly subjective and qualitative therefore risk measurement should be assessed in different contexts in the same application environment.

7.3.1.2 Understand Your Risk

An understanding of the risk and the level of the danger associated with it, is highly dependent on factors, such as the experience of the analyst, training, background and an understanding of the system being examined.

7.3.1.3 Set a Target for Your Risk

The risk target relates to potential areas which are likely to have elements of danger. This also suggests there should be an understanding of the information system and the environment within which it is deployed.

7.3.1.4 Manage Your Risk

This is the stage where vulnerabilities, threats and potential dangers are analysed together. A set of countermeasures are recommended as a means of mitigating the threats that might result in potential danger.

7.3.1.5 Adopt Standards

Adopting the appropriate standards is a way of certifying your information system. It is basically to ensure that minimum security requirements are put in place. There are a wide range of standards that one could adopt and tailor to a particular information system. The obvious one is the ISO17799, which was derived from the BS7799 for security management implementation, a defacto standard for the UK Government.

7.4   ASSET (Automatic Security Self Evaluation Tool) –
Nist(2002)

ASSET is designed with the primary objective of identifying a standard way of performing self assessment. This is done by using a self assessment guide which highlights questions directed at the system specific control objectives measured against a benchmark. It is designed to help system managers gather system data. The assessment process involves data collection, reporting and analysis. It speeds up the data collection and reporting processes, as a result supporting the assessment process. There are roles or processes actively played by actors. These actors are the manager or Chief Information Officer (CIO), collector, reporter and expert of the subject being considered.

7.5   JAVA Security Model

JAVA is a programming language. Its design is based on the object oriented paradigm and for meeting challenges in application development of heterogeneous and distributed network systems. JAVA security model is based on what is known as the sand box model.

7.5.1   Sandbox Model

The sandbox model has a dedicated area that allows untrusted code to run or execute on a system. This is not a familiar feature common to traditional operating systems. Its proponents argue in the literature that JAVA security model allows an applet to solely execute in the sandbox region and similar regions within the JAVA virtual machine (JVM). In other words malicious code could be protected. This however does not apply JAVA applications, since they are mostly bought off the shelf and installed on individual's or an organisation's PC. Within the perimeters of the sandbox is JAVA security manager. Its role is to ensure that borders of the sandbox is respected and observed. In the event of an applet performing maliciously, JAVA's virtual machine checks with the security manager if the running of an applet goes ahead. If the feedback is positive the code is allowed to run or else terminated. Common issues regarding this security model relates to authentication and encryption of data. It is also vulnerable to the "man in the middle attack". This attack is a description given to the interception of data by an agent on a network usually observing the communication between client/servers of a network. JAVA usually adopts a technique known as "digital shrinkwrapping" to counteract this form of attack. This is achieved by exposing tampering of responses sent from a server. It checks the integrity of the server's response. JAVA security model is effective and useful within the confines of the operating systems platform. The main weakness of the security model is that it does not take into account embedded and inherent risk within a communication network. Whiles the network platform promotes mobility it also exposes itself to numerous attacks on the network. Although development of the sandbox model extended to the entire JVM based on the thinking of "no built in notion of untrusted code to networks", the key risk highlighted which is common to networks, still hangs like a "debacle sword" on the JAVA security model Fritzinger S.J, Mueller M (1997).

7.6 Current Approaches and Trends in Security Management

7.6.1 HS - Holistic Security

The concept of holistic approach to information security was introduced by Williams (2003) within the context of both risk and security management on global communication platforms. This has been a prominent area of research with industry playing significant role, although within domains of advanced economies. Musaj (2006) proposes design steps believed to be key to creating holistic security. The enterprise architecture serves as the foundation of holistic security. Four layers are identified as components of the architecture. These are, Business Architecture (BA), Information Architecture (IA), Application Architecture (AA) and Technical Architecture (TA). The model seems to be based on non functional system requirements. These are requirements which when satisfied support the business processes of an organisation. The paper discusses technology requirements, which cut across different application environments and boundaries. The checklist comprises approximately 86 items related to security architecture design specification. Musaj (2006) argues that security is not a technological issue but a management one. Although this is true to some extent, we can not understate the fact that technology plays a vital role in the successful management of security.

7.6.2   ISMM - Information Security Maturity Model

According to Symantec, although information security is sometimes not the heart of most organisations competence, it is a central requirement of most organisations. ERP (Enterprise Resource Planning), TQM (Total Quality Management) and CMMI (Capability Maturity Model Integration) are frameworks, when implemented could serve as a base for serving a corporate information system Alaboodi Saad Saleh (2006). Alaboodi Saad Saleh (2006) place emphasis on the implementation of standards as a means of supporting technical security. There is importance placed on proactive rather than reactive approach. The author introduces a new Information security maturity model (ISMM) that incorporates different schools of thought in the security industry.

ISMM covers 3 main areas. These are layering dimension, process dimension and people dimension. The layering dimension describes five main areas. These are, 1 physical and environmental security, 2 front end system security, 3. backend system security, 4 comprehensive security awareness and 5 definite security. Each of these layers has strengths with regards to specific problem areas, covered within requirements of holistic security. The general notion of ISMM is that visibility decreases across the layer from physical and environment security to the last layer known as definite security. Although the model attempts to integrate security requirements and systems, there is no evidence and importance placed on risks captured during the application of the security models. The models solution areas map onto domains outlined by ISO17799 for security standards AlAboodi S.S (2006).

7.7   Summary

Chapter 7 reviewed classical and contemporary security risk models for governments and businesses. The feature common to these Models was that none of them addressed risk inherent and associated with heterogeneous and hetero-standard systems as mentioned in chapter 3. Models proposed are usually based on the premise that network infrastructure supporting business processes were homo-standard. There is also too much emphasis on hardware and software. Security risks associated with soft issues such as skills and vulnerabilities with consumers have not been addressed satisfactorily.

Chapter 8

Theoretical, Conceptual
and Empirical Foundations of SSTM
(SERVICE SERVER TRANSMISSION MODEL)

8.1   Introduction

This chapter presents the theoretical, philosophical and empirical foundations of a more robust and effective security risk model known as SSTM for managing security risk in Online Business. It also describes details of concepts and notations underpinning SSTM. The key concepts and notations described in this chapter comprise risk (r), RAS (Risk Access Spots), RIG (Risk Identification Grid), RISG (Risk Identification Solutions Grid), and Zones. This chapter provides the reader with justifications and reasoning behind SSTM of synchronising e-security methodology.

8.2   Theoretical Concepts

The concept of synchronization in distributed systems has been primarily applied to problem areas associated with time and events on communication networks across different geographical locations.

Synchronization is mainly to ensure that, times associated and recorded with respect to the occurrence of network events are valid. The event could either be a financial transaction involving the purchasing of an airline ticket or credit transfer to a particular bank account. This usually involves the synchronization of physical and logical clocks. The primary objective of this type of synchronization is to ensure consistency, avoid discrepancies and duplication during and after the transaction. Algorithms supporting these types of transactions have been discussed and proposed by Christian and Berkeley Coulouris (2001). Other algorithms for synchronizing distributed processes include interactive convergence algorithm (ICA) of Lamport and Melliar-Smith, fault tolerant midpoint algorithm of Lundelius-Lynch, Schneider's generalised protocol of clock synchronization and generalised clock synchronization protocol in isabelle/HOL.BV (2005).

Whiles previous works on synchronization focused on times and events, this work extends previous works by applying synchronization to security of global heterogeneous and hetero-standard systems by modelling the relationship of risk access spots (RAS) between advanced and developing economic platforms. It is hypothesised that this modelling will help secure the security gap between these economies in real life applications. The mathematical model synchronizes the risk and probable type of attacks associated with electronic security on distributed platforms across the globe. It forms the foundation of a new design approach for securing systems deployed on developing and advanced economies computer and communication network platforms. Arguments for the model and accompanied graphical representations have been published in the book synchronizing E-Security Williams (2004). The book also reviews the graphical models and associated descriptions as background information to the reader as discussed in Williams (2004). Experiments have been conducted using simulation techniques such as monte carlo technique to proof the validity and credibility of the mathematical model.

Global and Local Zones are identified using a location based algorithm engineered from the model. The model defines parameters and criteria for the location based algorithm of the mathematical model.

The modelling of the relationships has been based on essential variables derived from results of empirical studies published in previous work of Williams (2003). The framework below highlights the main sources of risk from studies on electronic banking on communication networks.

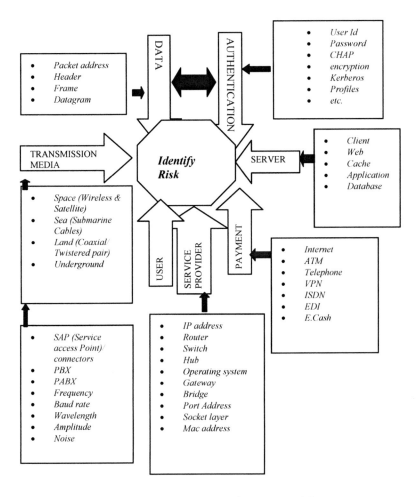

Figure 21 – Framework of SSTM model

The mathematical model uses basic set theory in conjunction with the Risk Identification Grid and Risk Identification and Solutions Grid in the synchronization process. The model is demonstrated as a simulation. The sources of risk identified are tabulated in the framework known as the RISG (Risk Identification and Solutions Grid. The Grid comprise risk identified an mapped unto appropriate solutions. The content of the risk identification framework may change depending on the application environment and the risk associated with that environment.

8.3   SSTM

SSTM is an integral part of the Synchronizing E-Security methodology based on the findings of empirical studies from the examination of communications infrastructure across the globe Williams (2004).

Previous models proposed by PMBOK (1996), Higuera and Haines (1996), Chapman and Ward (1997), Buchman (1994) and the integrated approach for risk response development in project planning by Ben-David and T. Raz (2001), OCTAVE, CRAMM, ASSET, JAVA security model and SCERT do not address security as an integral part of risk assessment, as SSTM adopts a holistic approach to risk and security management. This is the fundamental difference between Synchronisation E-Methodology using SSTM and previous Models.

This work presents the mathematical model as proof of concept and practical demonstration of the Service Server Transmission Model SSTM as a tool for synchronizing electronic risk and security methods. It is central to Synchronising E-Security Methodology originally published in the book Synchronising E-Security Williams (2003) mentioned in the background.

The analysis, evaluations and experimentations are based on seven risk areas within the selected risk access spots (RAS) identified in the SSTM of Synchronising E-Security Toolkit Williams (2003).

8.4   Reasons for SSTM

1. **Technologies that support electronic transactions are globally available to both advanced and developing economies Williams (2004).**

The global economy has technologies, which are available and accessible by both developing and advanced economies. There are also electronic commerce activities in both types of economies. The current technological age makes risk assessment of security in a global context a critical programme. There are Internet Users across the globe regardless of economic strength. Although the percentage of user participation of the Internet is not similar everywhere across the globe, there is evidence that developing economies have technologies that enable them to engage in electronic transactions similar to that of advanced economies. The author thinks that when it comes to the application of technology, mass or size does not matter much. A small mass of a certain type of technology can depict vulnerability that could be used as a means of attack.

2. **The weaknesses in security that exist in electronic fund transfer, Internet and Telephone Banking could be exploited by electronic criminals across the globe.**

This suggests that it is important to synchronise the communications infrastructure available to both developing and advanced economies. It has been advocated strongly in this text that synchronising security among economies is critical. The lack of synchronisation of these security platforms leaves a security gap. Hackers and intruders could exploit the gaps in security. The present gap can be harmonised by encouraging the appropriate standards and policies. Policies and standards should fit the economic structure of developing economies. Risk is relative and subjective. The risks associated with technologies in advanced economies are not the same as those in developing economies. These are important factors that every risk analyst, systems manager and information systems management consultant should be aware of.

3. **Risk assessment of authentication methods needs to be improved due to the lack of holistic approach in the design of security policies and standards. Certification processes in advanced economies do not integrate risks that evolve from developing economies.**

The rules that constitute the design of security policies and algorithms do not integrate risk factors that evolve from developing economies. This means those security software designs do not anticipate risks and vulnerability that might evolve from the Internet platforms of developing economies. It is time for designers and developers to investigate risk factors that might cause harm as a result of such weaknesses. Supposing we assume that the mindsets and profiles of electronic criminals are the same, it could be argued that, electronic crime in advanced economies are similar to ones in developing economies. Perhaps that is the rationale behind the design of existing security systems and methods. Although that might be true in some instances, in Synchronizing the platforms and means of access to vulnerable elements of communication technologies are very different as evidenced by empirical studies in synchronizing e-security Williams (2004). This means that the avenues of attack as a result of present risk related to the communication technologies of developing economies are more compared to that of advanced economies.

4. Growth of Online business in both developing and advanced economies has driven the need to employ security methods based on standards that reflect the current state of technology globally.

Current global electronic business trends show that e-trade is still on the rise although there have been instances of Dot Com failures. There is enthusiastic participation from developing economies. The arms of central governments, banks and private companies are being encouraged to take opportunity of the competitive advantage that comes with the participation in such ventures. In advanced economies at least 60 to 70% of the population participate in some form of Tele-banking or Internet banking. Customers check their current account balances via telephone or Internet. Similar percentages of people use their credit cards to purchase items on the Internet. All these activities form part of e-trading.

5. The synchronisation of e-security methods will loosen the chains of E-trade regulations in advanced economies and make it friendlier to developing economies.

Although regulations governing trade in advanced economies are not mandatory, it suggests that there are risk factors, which could only be borne by companies who choose to violate these regulations. E-trading will continue as technology becomes more sophisticated. For instance there are new mobile communication technologies that currently work in conjunction with the Internet using protocols such as (WAP) Wireless Application Protocol Keen, Mackintosh, (2001), WiFi, WiMAX and WLAN. These communication devices could be employed to outpace current risk prevention technologies. For instance mobile communication devices could be disabled at street market places and transferred to any part of the world. The software for carrying this task is readily available at street markets. Replacing electronic chips in these mobile devices with custom built electronic chips could be highly dangerous and risky to electronic security.

6. **Human vulnerabilities for both technical and non technical manpower leave much to be desired.**

The regional imbalance between developing and advanced economies needs to be addressed by channelling standards through organised bodies and structures such as governmental agencies, leading IT firms in these economies and interested academics. This could be achieved by both advanced and developing economies taking initiatives, which will be embraced by both economic communities. Such initiatives could be achieved through international conferences and forums with the participation of governments. Developing economies should be encouraged to contribute to discussions that lead to formulation of new ISO standards. For example how many representatives from Africa are in the committee for drafting the new ISO/IEC 24744 standard for software engineering meta-model for development methodologies? This is an area which western leaders in technology and associated governments including lobby groups of professional bodies have been quite inward looking with respect to standard development.

7. **Exponential rise and growth of global electronic risk.**

It is also likely that risk will increase due to a relative increase in capital expenditure in communication technologies in developing economies. The pace at which technologies are permanently distributed across the globe needs to be investigated and addressed with urgency. Lack of similar pace in the advancement of standards in information security management will cause a relative increase in security spending in advanced economies. The alternative means of solving the e-trade ban and regulations is by closing the gap in risk between advanced and developing economies.

Findings from empirical studies originally published in Williams (2004) depict that developing economies have placed less importance on risk spending. Although there are existing risks from the gap analysis conducted, there is still an increase in capital expenditure rather than risk mitigation technologies. The contrast shows that advanced economies over estimate risk.

Each of the steps discussed above will go a long way to help developing economies gain the credibility necessary for e-trading which will eventually reduced risk globally. It may also increase investment drive in developing economies in the medium term. This will ultimately have an effect on global economic productivity.

Current risk methodologies in information systems do not address this gap that exists which needs synchronisation.

A methodology has been proposed for synchronising e-security methods in global electronic transactions in the next section.

8.5   Descriptions of SSTM of Synchronizing E-Security Methodology

This section is a description of Synchronising E-Security Methodology. There are six levels in the implementation process of the Methodology. These are usually accompanied by a set of models, known as SSTM (Service Server Transmission Model) presented below.

Level 1

Risk identification is the process of randomly listing areas considered to be risk access spots within the information system or network communication platform. Risk identification could span from areas as generically represented at levels 1 and 2 of the methodology.

This is the first step in the e-synchronisation process. Identifying the risk from risk access spots is the approach adopted by this methodology. Risk spots in italics might not necessarily be risk access spots in every environment although the view taken by this book has been derived from findings of field studies. This might vary from one environment to the other. It is however recommended that these risk access spots are used as a basic guide when accessing risk spots in any online business environment application environment.

Level 2

The objective of this level is to build a trail of perceived risk in the application environment. This could range from online banking, gaming, electronic payment system, general practitioner information system, online video service or online stock and inventory systems for a wholesale or delivery service. The risk identified should be extracted and well documented.

Level 3

(RIG) Risk Identification Grid extracted from **levels 1 and 2**. The grid shows recommended risk access spots on a network. The RIG was based on risk spots common to both developing and advanced economies operating and networks platforms identified in empirical studies by Williams (2004). The security analyst could make changes to the RIG by editing risks that are particularly associated with specific problems or application environments.

Level 4

This is risk integration. The process of identifying common and uncommon risk across all network platforms. This step is critical to the success of the synchronisation process. It involves the process of identifying common and uncommon risk across all network platforms. This step is critical to the success of the synchronisation process.

Level 5

This is the process of auditing the risk. This stage subjects the risks to an assessment, which determines whether risk is perceived or actual. A perceived risk is a risk which is judged as potential threat. An actual risk is a risk judged to be a threat. The auditing at this level is meant to make the type of risk clear. This can be derived using the SSTM mathematical model for calculating risk.

Level 6

This is (RISG) Risk Identification and Solution Grid. This grid shows recommended RAS on a network with suggested solutions from a software simulator. The RISG is based on recommended solutions provided by a security expert or the simulator. Synchronizing E-Security Toolkit comes with a set of solutions.

Fundamental Concepts of (SSTM) Service Server Transmission Model of
Synchronising E-Security Methodology.

The ideas central to Synchronising E-security Methodology are based
SSTM comprising risk identification, extraction, integration, audit and a
risk identification solution grid derived from risk access spots on network
and operating system platforms.

8.6   Pictorial Representation of SSTM

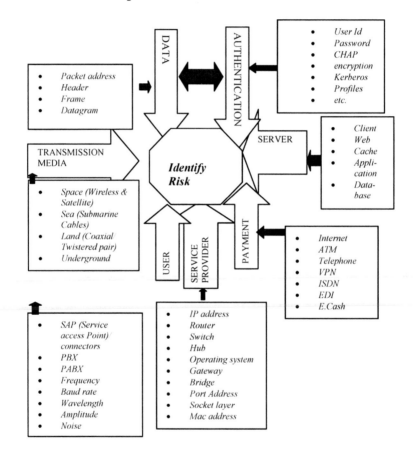

Figure 22 – LEVEL 1 - SSTM – (SERVICE SERVER TRANSMISSION MODEL)
of Synchronizing E-Security

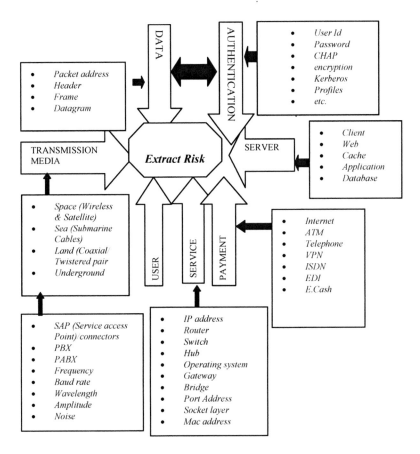

Figure 23 – LEVEL 2 - SSTM – (SERVICE SERVER TRANSMISSION MODEL) of Synchronizing E-Security

	Z7	Z6	Z5	Z4	Z3	Z2	Z1
Z1	IP-Address	Bandwith	Baudrate	Switch	Hub	Location	Skill
Z2	Router	Packet address	ATM	E-cash	EDI	VPN	Satellite
Z3	Wavelength	Earth station	VPN	OSS	E-Chip	Terminator	Gateway
Z4	USER	SAP	PBX	Cyphertext	Password	Socket layer	Repeater
Z5	Sec. Provider	Amplitude	Application	Profile	Cable/Wire	Connectors	Frame
Z6	Noise	ISP	Web Server	Dbase Server	Cache Server	Frequency	Router
Z7	Circuit	Protocol	Datagram	MAC address	Port address	SAP (Service Access Provider)	Client Server

Figure 24 – LEVEL 3 - (RIG) Risk Identification Grid

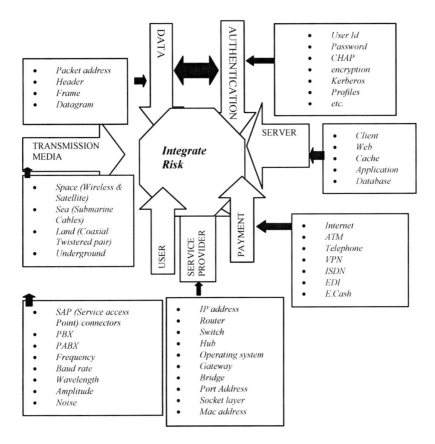

Figure 25 – LEVEL 4 - SSTM – (SERVICE SERVER TRANSMISSION MODEL)
of Synchronizing E-Security

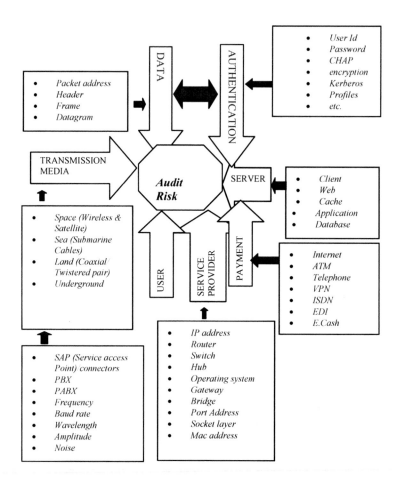

Figure 26 – LEVEL 5 - SSTM – (SERVICE SERVER TRANSMISSION MODEL)
of Synchronizing E-Security

	Z1	Z2	Z3	Z4	Z5	Z6	Z7
Z1	Skill	Location	Hub	Switch	Baudrate	Bandwith	IP-Address
Z2	Satellite	VPN	EDI	E-cash	ATM	Packet address	Router
Z3	Gateway	Terminator	E-Chip	OSS	VPN	Earth station	Wavelength
Z4	Repeater	Socket layer	Password	Cyphertext	PBX	SAP	USER
Z5	Frame	Connectors	Cable/Wire	Profile	Application	Amplitude	Sec. Provider
Z6	Router	Frequency	Cache Server	Dbase Server	Web Server	ISP	Noise
Z7	Client Server	SAP (Service Access Provider)	Port address	MAC address	Datagram	Protocol	Circuit

SOLUTIONS

Figure 27 – LEVEL 6 - (RISG) Risk Identification Solution Grid

8.7   Guidelines for Using the Model

- **Integrate risk preventive technologies**

It is essential that current technologies available for risk prevention should be available to both advanced and developing economies. There should be a clear understanding of importance associated with risk preventive technologies. The design aspects should also integrate characteristics that foresee risk from both developing and advanced economies perspectives. Software designed for risk prevention should have the capability to analyse risk factors that take into account socio cultural elements in developing economies. There is the need to adopt a context based approach to risk, by integrating such factors.

- **Prioritise global technology scheme**

Newly developed technologies should be based on schemes that address fundamental bottlenecks of risk preventive technologies. For instance examine whether training schemes that support technology take a holistic approach, by putting into perspective training needs of developing economies vis-à-vis advance economies.

- **Prioritise national and international funding for technologies**

Funding that support any form of technological development should be properly prioritised. The scale of preference of such prioritisation should be based on an understanding of the risk requirements in specific economies. The need for a context based approach is paramount and a critical success factor.

- **Verify premature distribution of hardware and software across the globe**

Manufacturing and distribution of hardware and software should not be executed prematurely. Vendors of hardware and software should verify whether products being marketed meet minimum security requirements such as the C2 classification of the orange books. The buyers of these technologies should revalidate and reassess whether the products being sold to them meet security requirements that are globally acceptable. A thorough examination of security features should be beta tested by the user.

- **Ensure that certification of software and hardware is satisfactory**

Certification should be managed and delivered thorough the appropriate set of controls or framework recommended and well understood by users. Certification should provide the assurance and trust that organisations need to forge ahead business security. Addressing and predicting uncertainties that might evolve in different environments should be embodied in security model implementation. The integrity of the certifier for information assurance should be verified.

- **Reconcile the disparities in skills of human ware within the environment the technology will be implemented**

Train technical and non technical manpower that interact or communicate with the technology. Training is the engine to growth and sustainability. Most developing economies lack the necessary infrastructure to support in house training within organisations. There is also a lack of appreciation regarding the role that training play in developing personnel whether at operational, tactical or strategic level. Training schemes adopted within developing economies are more structured compared with advanced economies. Advanced economies therefore have the flexibility to easily adopt different trading models.

- **Refuse to be misdirected by the "Bandwagon syndrome"**

Do not be led. Take the lead in the introduction of any technology or information system. Before an introduction of new technology in your environment or organisation, a thorough assessment should be made to establish whether such a technology is required. The assessment can also determine the best strategy for optimising technical and non technical resources.

8.8   General Concepts

This section introduces a number of concepts that explains the techniques and notations adopted by the models of the methodology. The following are concepts central to the methodology: (RAS) Risk Access Spots introduced as a footnote in section (RIG) Risk Identification Grid, (RISG) Risk Identification Solutions Grid and (Z) Zones.

8.8.1   Risk

An event that poses a threat or danger to a computer system and communication network. It is also the value or importance attached to a network vulnerability.

Ben-David and T. Raz (2001) also define it as the exposure to the probability that an event with adverse consequences might occur. In other words an event that has a negative effect on the normality of a system.

8.8.2   (RAS) Risk Access Spots

RAS are areas of risk that could be perceived, actual or emerge as a hoax and may be vulnerable to threat or attack. Identifying RAS is the first level of the methodology. RAS are not permanent, although certain areas could be recommended as risk prone than others. RAS are dynamic and might not necessarily follow any particular pattern. The identification of RAS should be followed by risk extraction. Extracting the risk and documenting the risk is essential to providing solutions. The risk extracts are documented using the (RIG) Risk Identification Grid.

8.8.3   Zones

Zones are demarcated areas where risk could be perceived or emerge. Synchronising E-Security methodology proposes seven Zones as hypothetical risk regions. The proposition is based on the notion that RAS emerge at different levels of network and operating systems, which support international, national, city, town, company or organisation's electronic activity. The least divisible part of a zone is a node (n) on a communication network. A node has parameters or variables which are synchronized during synchronization. These include time, risk, event and attack history.

A zone can also comprise many processes. This could be represented as, $Z = (P_1 \ldots \ldots P_n)$, where P is a process in a zone and P_n. is infinite number of processes. Every zone (z) is associated with both physical and logical clock, which is a characteristic of most synchronization primitives and algorithms. The logical clock is a derivative of physical clock in any geographical location. The physical clocks are adjusted due to drift times and rates associated with physical clocks. Each process in a zone is responsible for reading risks® associated with that process. In order words, there is one to one, one to many, or many to many relationships between zones (z) and processes.

8.8.4 (RIG) Risk Identification Grid

RIG is a two-dimensional array grid comprising RAS and (Z) Zones. The risk access spots identified on RIG is integrated. The purpose of the integration is to determine common and non-common risk amongst the seven Zones in the RIG which represent network and operating system platforms in any geographical region. The process of risk integration is followed by a risk audit, which creates a synthesis of perceived and actual risk. Solutions are then provided for the actual risk whiles contingencies are put in place to monitor the perceived risk using the RISG. An expert or the proposed simulator in this text could be consulted to deal with the RAS documented in the RIG. The concepts that drive Synchronising E-Security Methodology have been modelled using (SSTM) Service Server Transmission Model.

	Z7	Z6	Z5	Z4	Z3	Z2	Z1
Z1	IP-Address	Bandwith	Baudrate	Switch	Hub	Location	Skill
Z2	Router	Packet address	ATM	E-cash	EDI	VPN	Satellite
Z3	Wavelength	Earth station	VPN	OSS	E-Chip	Terminator	Gateway
Z4	USER	SAP	PBX	Cyphertext	Password	Socket layer	Repeater
Z5	Sec. Provider	Amplitude	Application	Profile	Cable/Wire	Connectors	Frame
Z6	Noise	ISP	Web Server	Dbase Server	Cache Server	Frequency	Router
Z7	Circuit	Protocol	Datagram	MAC address	Port address	SAP (Service Access Provider)	Client Server

RIG - Risk Identification Grid – Level 3 of SSTM

8.8.5   Local Zone

The location refers to a network area within a radius of 100meters. It is location where an event or attack takes place within the 100meters radius.

8.8.6   Global Zone

A network area or radius which is outside 100 meters demarcation This covers all locations affected due to an event or attack on a local zone.

8.8.7   Zone Grading

A zone is graded at different threat or risk levels as a result of an association with a RAS within a zone. For example networks deployed in developing economies within the larger context of global network infrastructure, such as the Internet suffer a higher risk. This make such networks pose more danger to global networks. Risks associated with RAS are graded as 1, 2, 3 where 1 is Low, 2 is medium and 3 is High. It is important to note that a RAS graded as 1 in a particular zone could be graded as 3 in another zone. This primarily depends on location, although there are other factors that come to play.

8.8.8   Sync

Sync represents α (alpha) as the synchronisation primitive that manages the asynchronous nature of risks and attacks on computer networks located at different zones.

8.8.9   Time

The time an attack or event took place. This is important since time zones vary globally, as such capturing the time of such an attack or event is essential to profiling when such attacks and events are likely to take place. Whiles a physical time is derived from a physical clock in a geographical location. A logical time is derived from a logical clock.

8.8.10 Event

An event is any system activity that is likely to generate a system response, although not all responses from the system is visible or measurable by a computer security management system. It is also an anomaly to system activities. This book takes the view that events can be generated accidentally or deliberately. An event also triggers a computer network or system response, visible and non visible to a network administration and management system and associated with a **RAS**.

8.8.11 Attack

Any activity that exploits risk access spots with the goal of breaching security. An attack is an event with catastrophic consequences, whether deliberate or accidental. Its source may be known or concealed. The nature of a network attack is analogous to an act of war. It has no pre-defined rules like a road traffic system. Its demographic relationship is non correlated. However there are functional variables when captured could serve as a guide to expected attacks, based on risks whether known or unknown.

8.8.12 (RISG) – Risk Identification Solutions Grid

Risk Identification Solutions Grid denotes mapping between risk access spots identified within the zones and recommended solutions, which in some cases could be described as countermeasures prescribed to mitigate the risk flagged to be a threat or danger. The RISG is the point where the outcome of the risk assessment is integrated with appropriate security solutions embedded within the RISG Simulator. The countermeasures or solutions drawn can also originate from a human expert as part of the solutions that the RISG simulator provides.

Risk Identification Solution Grid Level 6

	Z7	Z1	Z2	Z3	Z4	Z5	Z6
Z1	IP-Address	Skill	Location	Hub	Switch	Baudrate	Bandwith
Z2	Router	Satellite	VPN	EDI	E-cash	ATM	Packet address
Z3	Wavelength	Gateway	Terminator	E-Chip	OSS	VPN	Earth station
Z4	USER	Repeater	Socket layer	Password	Cypher-text	PBX	SAP
Z5	Sec. Provider	Frame	Connectors	Cable/Wire	Profile	Application	Amplitude
Z6	Noise	Router	Frequency	Cache Server	Dbase Server	Web Server	ISP
Z7	Circuit	Client Server	SAP (Service Access Provider)	Port address	MAC address	Datagram	Protocol

SOLUTIONS
Level 6 of SSTM - (RISG) Risk Identification and Solution Grid

8.9   Symbolic and Mathematical Notations

This section presents a mathematical model and notations underlying SSTM (Service Server Transmission Model) as well as general description of the model. There are six levels which form the implementation section and process of the models linked to the methodology.

1. Lest Risk notations be represented as:

r = risk
Ir = risk identification
Er = risk extraction
Ir → Er = RIG (Risk Identification Grid)
Int = risk integration (common & uncommon risk)

2. Let Synchronisation primitive be represented as Sync = α

3. Let Time & Event Notations be represented as:

t = time
e = event
z = local zone
Z = Global zone
γ = attack

4. Generic relational notations

We present the relationship between r, x, y, z, Z, γ *as*

$\alpha = r \rightarrow t \rightarrow e \rightarrow z \rightarrow Z \rightarrow \gamma$ or $r \cap t \cap e \cap z$

5. We represent $z \rightarrow Z$ *as* $z \subseteq Z$ (z is a subset Z) and $z \subset Z$ (not a proper subset of Z)

6. According to SSTM Probability of risk r is calculated as $P_B = ((Z^n) +$ time t + event e) x sync **α / cost**

Global and Local Zones are identified using a location and profile based algorithm engineered from the model. The model defines parameters and criteria for locating risk, threat and possible attack.

8.10   Graphical Notations

1.

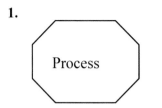

Security risk analyser and processor

2.

Security risk access spot indicator

3.

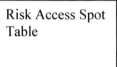

Specifies details of RAS (Risk Access Spots) indicated by risk access spot flow diagram

4.

Risk Access Spot flow

8.11   Summary

This chapter provided an insight into the risk spots and security vulnerabilities of information systems that support Online Business and electronic based transactions. The methodology proposed highlights the fact that there are risk access spots that need to be identified in the development process of such systems. It also suggests the need to determine perceived risk and actual risk. Although the risks identified are of critical importance to such systems, the risk areas could evolve or change. The underlying mathematical model is applied to electronic business cases with regards to on-line banking and results presented in chapter 9.

The chapter also described details of concepts and notations underpinning SSTM. The Concepts and notations described comprised, risk, (r), RAS (Risk Access Spots), Zones, which represents Locations on a network. Zones can be local or global. They are graded as 1, 2 and 3 meaning low, medium and high levels. RIG (Risk Identification Grid) for integrating risk extracted during risk assessment. Factors essential to synchronization process were outlined. These include time, event and attack, as well as the Zone. RISG (Risk Identification and Solutions Grid) a tabulation of recommended solutions for the security risk problem identified in RIG was also presented. A subsection of the chapter recaptured guidelines for implementing SSTM.

Chapter 9

Simulating SSTM Using Monte Carlo

9.1   Introduction

This chapter provides a simulation of SSTM using case scenarios. The purpose of the simulations is to assess the reliability and trustworthiness of the model in assessing security risk in Online Business Security for heterogeneous and hetero-standard systems with respect to communication networks using Monte Carlo method.

9.2   General Problem Scenario

In this scenario we will attempt to predict possible events likely to occur using SSTM and verify them by Monte Carlo method.

The general problem scenario is based on the following set of questions:

1. How is the security of an organisation with a local and global network infrastructure assessed?

2. How do such risks threaten the confidentiality, integrity and availability of its information services?

3. Supposing an activity on a network with parameters x_1 to x_n is identified in a particular geographical location of the network platform, what will be the probability of risk?

The need to model and simulate security risks across such network platforms strengthens our understanding of sources and nature of risks faced by organisations which have local, metropolitan and global business presence.

9.3   Overview of Monte Carlo

Monte Carlo is a method for risk analysis and uncertainty. It simulates real life systems. Monte Carlo uses random numbers and probability to evaluate structured and non structured problems. Monte Carlo method has been used extensively for modelling and simulating problems similar to the model being tested, due to its ability to randomise set of activities. In general, the steps involved in Monte Carlo simulation are as follows:

1. Create a parameter based model

- A model is created comprising parameters or attributes of the model being built. This can be represented in mathematical form as security risk = $f(x)$, where $f(x)$ is a function with elements x_1 to x_n

2. Create a set of random inputs $(x_i 1, x_i 2, x_i 3 \ x_i 4 \ x_i \ n)$

- Different security risk scenarios are generated for input into the model being simulated

3. Test the model

- Model is tested using input variables

4. Save the results from the testing

- Results from the test is saved for comparative analysis

5. Analyse the results to establish confidence in the solution model

- Results are compared to other solutions models to establish significance of model

6. Repeat test for model

1000 security risk scenarios have been randomly generated as part of an experiment to evaluate SSTM. A random number in the series represents a security risk scenario.

9.4   Methodology for Testing SSTM

9.4.1   Research Method

The method applied in simulating the model is Monte Carlo.

9.4.2   Sources of Data

Initial sources of data for simulation have been extracted from the following sources:

Risk Identification Grid (RIG) based on empirical studies Williams (2004).

Analysis of RAS generated using SSTM from case studies (Reliable sources)

9.4.3   Factors Likely to Affect Outcome of Analysis on Risk Access Spot

9.4.3.1 Types of data variables

- Time (local, global)
- Event (local, global)
- Attack (local, remote)
- Zone - Geographical location

9.4.4   Sensitivity Analysis

A method for refining data gathered through the fact finding exercise identifying factors critical to network security.

9.4.5   Fact Finding Methods Applied

Observation
Document sampling (independent records)
Interviews
Case studies
Empirical studies

9.4.6   Factors Considered in Determining Accuracy of Data Collected

Pessimistic and optimistic views expressed by personnel providing information about existing network infrastructure. Security policy of governments is a useful source of data if available.

9.5   Application of SSTM in Case Studies

This section is a description of case scenarios where SSTM has been applied in real life environments. The section illustrates the application of the
model in security risk assessment. Due to data protection and security
requirements of the companies which volunteered for this study, some
companies' names have been changed.

(CASE 1) - **Joint Logic Ltd VoIP**

Joint Logic Ltd introduced Voice over IP (VoIP). There have been concerns
with regards to security. In a more general sense this is how the company's
VoIP work. Voice over Internet Protocol (VoIP) is a technology that enables phone calls using the Internet. It virtually costs nothing. The Internet
transfers information in the form of packets. In other words it is a packet
switching system. Supposing there are two points of communication on the
Internet called points A and B, the data sent from A to B is broken down
into packets. The address of B is then added to the start of each packet. The
packet-switching network despatches the packets to B by any route accessible on the network. Since each packet has the identifier of the intended
destination, a single communication channel can carry packets from different sources to different destinations. VoIP converts the sound which is
analogue to digital data. This digital signal (DATA) is placed into packets
for subsequent transmission on the Internet.

Although this technology is cheaper and is likely to be more efficient in the future, there are a number of issues and challenges that have not yet been overcome. Some of these issues are: Sound quality (The effect of noise and attenuation), Jitter (The variation in the time between packets arriving), Latency (The delay on a phone line) and Security. The company showed concerns with regards to confidentiality, integrity and availability of data. The company desires that such fears are alleviated before it gets out of hand. The company requires a risk assessment of this technology. The VoIP architecture formed the bedrock of this assessment.

LEVEL 1 - Identify Risk

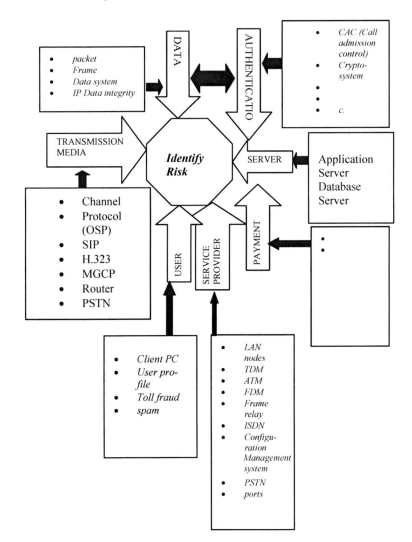

LEVEL 2 - Extract Risk

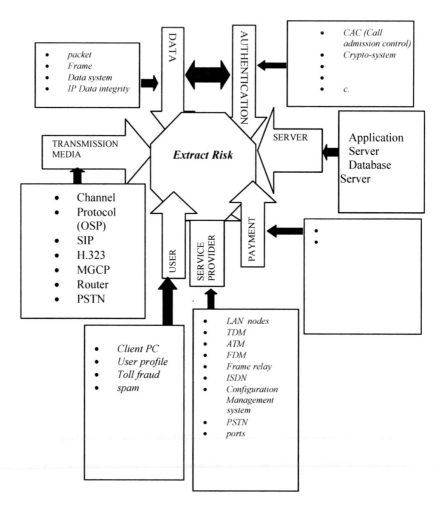

- CAC (Call admission control)
- Crypto-system
- •
- •
- c.

- packet
- Frame
- Data system
- IP Data integrity

DATA

AUTHENTICATION

TRANSMISSION MEDIA

Extract Risk

SERVER

Application Server Database Server

- Channel
- Protocol (OSP)
- SIP
- H.323
- MGCP
- Router
- PSTN

USER

SERVICE PROVIDER

PAYMENT

- •
- •

- Client PC
- User profile
- Toll fraud
- spam

- LAN nodes
- TDM
- ATM
- FDM
- Frame relay
- ISDN
- Configuration Management system
- PSTN
- ports

LEVEL 3 - (RIG) Risk Identification Grid

	Z1	Z2	Z3	Z4	Z5	Z6	Z7
Z1	Packet	Channel	Client PC	LAN Modes	Application Server	CAC	
Z2	Frame	Protocol	User Profile	TDM	Database Server	Crypto system	
Z3	Data System	SIP	Toll Fraud	ATM			
Z4	IP datagram	H.323	Spam	Frame relay			
Z5	MGCP	Ports	ISDN				
Z6	Router	Configuration System					
Z7	PSTN						

LEVEL 4 - Integrate Risk

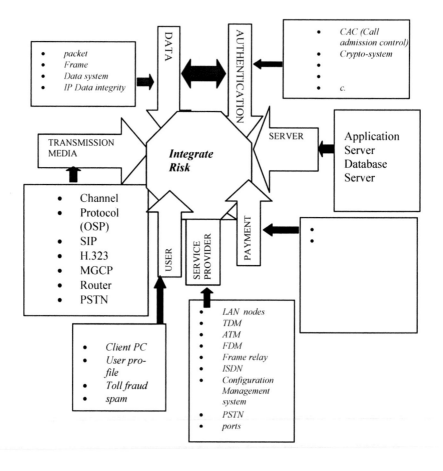

Level - 5 Audit Risk

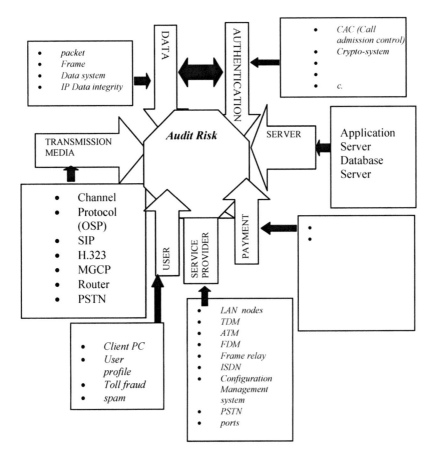

LEVEL 6 - (RISG) Risk Identification Solution Grid

	Z1	Z2	Z3	Z4	Z5	Z6	Z7
Z1	Packet	Frame	IP datagram / Data System	H.323	MGCP	Router	PSTN
Z2	Channel	Protocol	SIP	Spam	Ports	Configuration System	
Z3	Client PC	User Profile	Toll Fraud	Frame relay	ISDN		
Z4	LAN Modes	TDM	ATM				
Z5	Application Server	Database Server					
Z6	CAC	Crypto system					
Z7							

SOLUTIONS

(CASE 2) - **James Brown Healthcare (JBH)**

James Brown Healthcare (JBH) Technologies provides clinical and diag-
nostic workflow software and Internet services for pathology, laboratory
and radiology services enabling collaboration among physicians and clini-
cians and care settings. Recently James Brown Healthcare has decided to
move into the Application Service Provider (ASP) market; with the objective that they will have the capability to offer securely delivered clinical
data and applications to physicians, hospital workers and clients anywhere
in the world via the internet. As both a software vendor and ASP, JBH has
taken a proactive approach to contract a security consulting firm to assess
the risk that will enable them achieve JBH security goals.

LEVEL 1 - Identify Risk

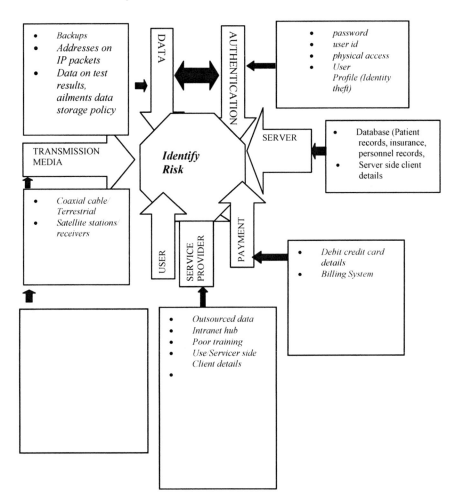

LEVEL 2 - Extract Risk

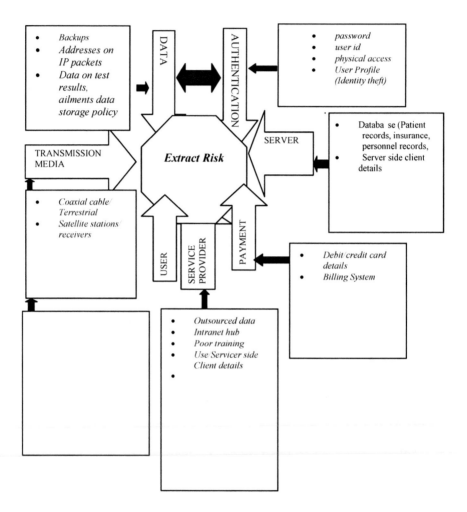

- Backups
- Addresses on IP packets
- Data on test results, ailments data storage policy

DATA

AUTHENTICATION

- password
- user id
- physical access
- User Profile (Identity theft)

TRANSMISSION MEDIA

Extract Risk

SERVER

- Databa se (Patient records, insurance, personnel records, Server side client details

- Coaxial cable/ Terrestrial
- Satellite stations/ receivers

USER

SERVICE PROVIDER

PAYMENT

- Debit/credit card details
- Billing System

- Outsourced data
- Intranet hub
- Poor training
- Use/Servicer side Client details
-

LEVEL 3 - (RIG) Risk Identification Grid

	Z1	Z2	Z3	Z4	Z5	Z6	Z7
Z1	Backups	IP address	Medical Data	Storage Policy			
Z2	Coaxial	Satellite	Receivers	Transmitters			
Z3	Out-sourced data						
Z4	Debit cards	Credit cards	Billing System	User Profile			
Z5	passwords	User id	Physical Access control				
Z6							
Z7							

LEVEL 4 - Integrate Risk

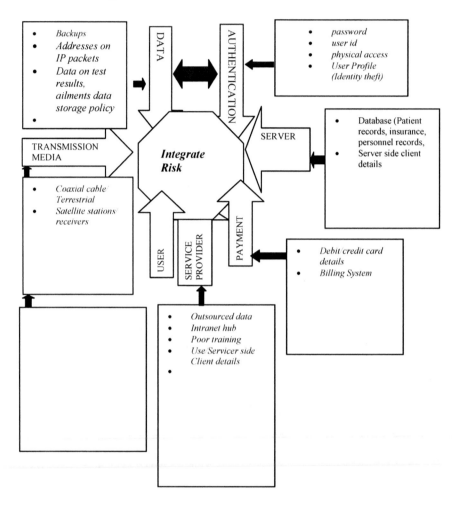

LEVEL 5 - Audit Risk

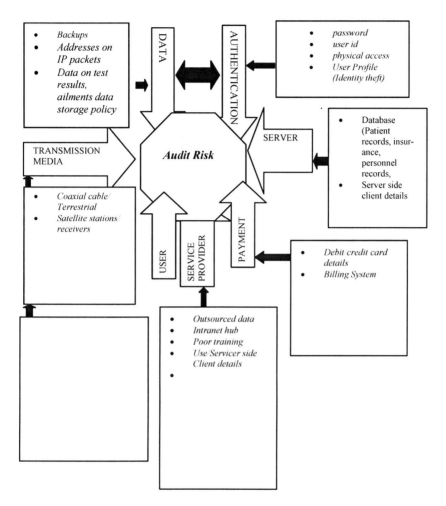

LEVEL 6 - (RISG) Risk Identification Solution Grid

	Z1	Z2	Z3	Z4	Z5	Z6	Z7
Z1	Backups	IP address	Medical Data	Storage Policy			
Z2	Coaxial	Satellite	Receivers	Transmitters			
Z3	Out-sourced data						
Z4	Debit cards	Credit cards	Billing System				
Z5	passwords	User id	Physical Access control	User Profile			
Z6							
Z7							

SOLUTIONS

(CASE 3) - **Sahara Ltd Internet Service Provider (ISP)**

"Sahara" is a medium-sized consultancy company with a strong focus on the development of specialist software solutions for their clients. Most clients are companies and institutions with specific structure or non-standard business models that off-the-shelf software (such as a standard ERP system) does not cater for. Typical clients are the governmental tax office, customs offices, police departments, and banks. These clients have strong requirements with respect to the security of their information flow. Clients pay for consultancy and a fee for the software installation at their premises.

Recently, Sahara decided to study a new business model for their company. They have decided to sell services instead of the software. This means that the software is not installed at the client's site, but that it is installed (and maintained) at Sahara's computer centre. The client uses the Internet to connect to and use these services. This approach has many advantages, most important of which is the long-term business relation between Sahara and it's clients. Other advantages are: ease of maintenance, sharing of code (e.g. all police departments run the same software with their own data space), guaranteed with respect to performance, availability, security and continuity planning.

Up till now, Sahara had no security model but the management is aware of the potential danger of using the Internet as a go-between. They request a couple of external security experts to study all security risks issues involved in this new business model.

LEVEL 1 – Identify Risk

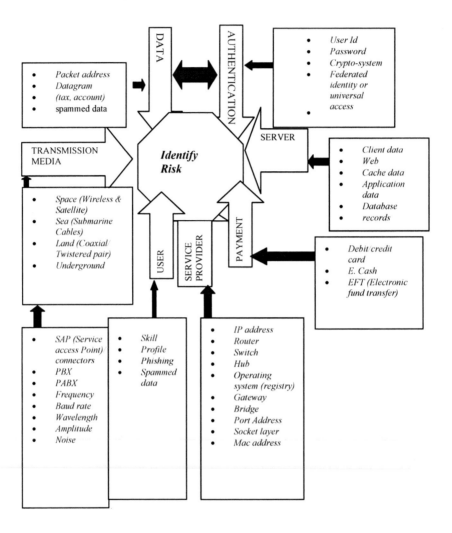

LEVEL 2 - Extract Risk

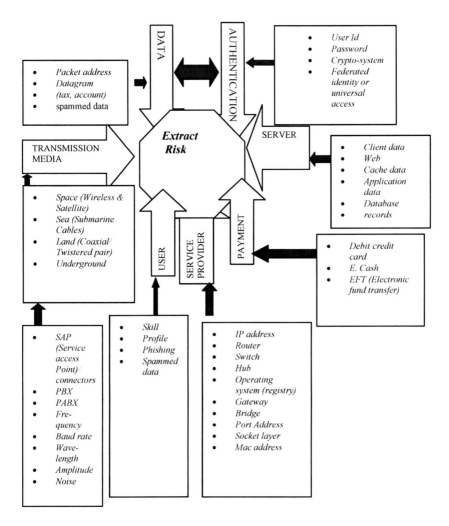

LEVEL 3 - (RIG) Risk Identification Grid

Z7	Z6	Z5	Z4	Z3	Z2	Z1	
IP-Address	Bandwith	Baudrate	Switch	Hub	Location	Skill	Z1
Router	Packet address	ATM	E-cash	EDI	VPN	Satellite	Z2
Wavelength	Earth station	VPN	OSS	E-Chip	Terminator	Gateway	Z3
USER	SAP	PBX	Cypher-text	Password	Socket layer	Repeater	Z4
Sec. Provider	Amplitude	Application	Profile	Cable/Wire	Connectors	Frame	Z5
Noise	ISP	Web Server	Dbase Server	Cache Server	Frequency	Router	Z6
Circuit	Protocol	Datagram	MAC address	Port address	SAP (Service Access Provider)	Client Server	Z7

LEVEL 4 - Integrate Risk

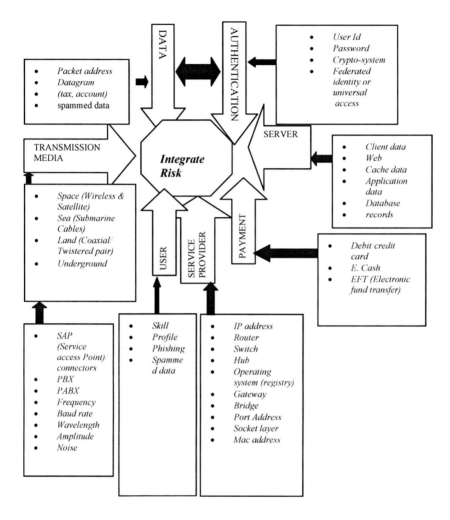

LEVEL 5 - Audit Risk

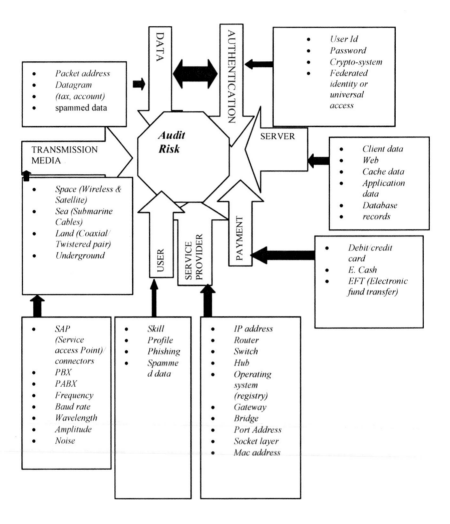

LEVEL 6 - (RISG) Risk Identification Solution Grid

Z1	Z2	Z3	Z4	Z5	Z6	Z7
Skill	Location	Hub	Switch	Baudrate	Bandwith	IP-Address
Satellite	VPN	EDI	E-cash	ATM	Packet address	Router
Gateway	Terminator	E-Chip	OSS	VPN	Earth station	Wavelength
Repeater	Socket layer	Password	Cypher-text	PBX	SAP	USER
Frame	Connectors	Cable/Wire	Profile	Application	Amplitude	Sec. Provider
Router	Frequency	Cache Server	Dbase Server	Web Server	ISP	Noise
Client Server	SAP (Service Access Provider)	Port address	MAC address	Datagram	Protocol	Circuit

SOLUTIONS

(CASE 4) - **Electronic Payment System in Sudan**

This case assesses the feasibility of the implementation of electronic payment system in Sudan by conducting a risk assessment on existing infrastructure, looking at the human and organisational factors among stakeholders. The field studies were carried jointly with Hesham my postgraduate dissertation student.

CASE STUDY - Electronic Payment System in Sudan (Feasibility Assessment Using SSTM Risk Assessment and Security Model)

Introduction

The overall banking policy between 1999 and 2002 of the Central Bank of Sudan considered computerising the banking sector to be the fundamental part of the policy, as a response to the millennium bug in year 2000. The level of computerization prior to this stage was the responsibility of individual banks. As part of this banking sector policy it was compulsory for these standard measures to be implemented. Mr. Sabir Mohamed Al-Hassan (The Governor of the Central Bank) stated that: The Central Bank compelled the commercial banks to connect their branches through networks. The Central Bank also completed the infrastructure required to connect the commercial banks with the central bank. It is now possible for a customer to check his or her account, or have a transaction processed from any branch.

A report issued by the Central Bank of Sudan in 2006 assessing the performance of the central bank of Sudan indicates that banking technology has been an essential part of the control process. It also reported that the use of the magnetic cheque has improved and simplified financial transactions.

The challenges faced by the Central Bank of Sudan were mainly economical, cultural or technical. As part of the feasibility studies risk assessment was carried out using SSTM.

Results from Fact Finding

The fact finding served as the basis for collecting data required for the risk assessment process. This questionnaire was designed to measure the readiness of the Sudanese population to welcome the E-Payment system. It is divided into two parts, the first part was distributed inside Sudan, and the second was distributed among Sudanese citizens who lived outside Sudan and already benefiting from E-Payment. The respondents were 61% students, 23% professional, 11% businesses, and 4% others. The youngest respondent was 17 years old, and the oldest was 67. The age groups of the respondents were classified as follows (less than 18) 7%, (18 to 25) 52%, (26 to 34) 21%, (34+) 16%, and 4% unspecified. The analysis of part one is as follows:

The questionnaire was designed in such a way that it assessed the feasibility of E-Payment system implementation in Sudan from the users' point of view.

The analysis of the results indicated that 77% of the respondents inside Sudan do not have Bank accounts; most of them gave trust reasons, while 100% of the respondents outside Sudan had Bank accounts, Credit or Debit Cards. The majority of them, both inside and out side Sudan, think it is beneficial, easy to use, or the easiest way to make payment. However, they expressed their concern about privacy, security, and availability. Knowledge is a key factor as it prevented 81% of the respondents inside Sudan from accessing the Internet, whereas it prevented 33% of the respondents outside Sudan from having online banking accounts. It was not the greatest preventative factor, if online risk is taken into account, as it prevents 57% of them from benefiting from online banking. Their response to the role of government question was not impressive as 63% did not give reasons.

The questionnaire is meant to investigate the popularity of the banking industry. Amongst the respondents "trust" was a major issue as well as their knowledge about E-Payment systems. The study also examined their ability to adapt to new technology, and the impact of the digital divide.

Using SSTM

Some components of SSTM are modified to match this study. For example it used Data Centre instead of Service Provider, because the data centre of the central bank of Sudan is the focus of this study, this saved the Server's entity as it will be used as a RAS at the Data Centre entity. Instead we added "Service" entity, which included "Connection points", "Infrastructure", "Application", "Training", "Skill", and Customer Service. Also we identified RAS associated with "User" and "Data", as results of the questionnaire showed increasing concern with respect to privacy of personal data, knowledge, and trust.

Level 1 - Identifying the risk

Below are the risks identified from the fact finding results after applying SSTM at level 1. This is the first step where risks are identified from Risk Access Spots (RAS). The original model does not have RAS at user, or Data levels.

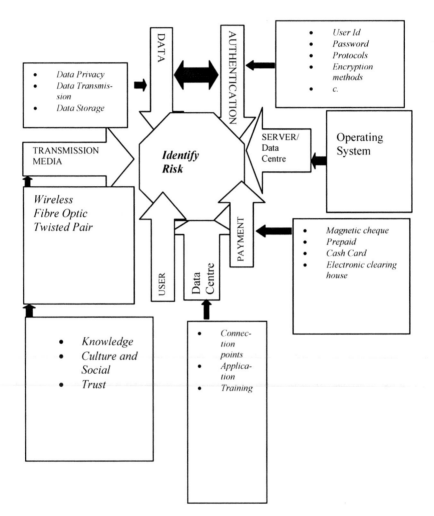

LEVEL 2 - Extract Risk

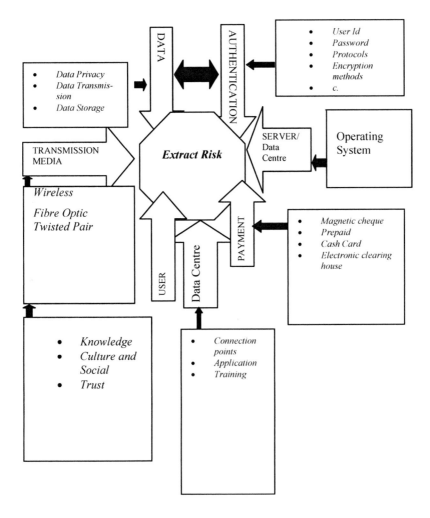

LEVEL 3 - (RIG) Risk Identification Grid

	Z1	Z2	Z3	Z4	Z5	Z6	Z7
Z1	knowledge	skill	configuration	Applications	Operating System		
Z2	Training	Trust	User ID	Protocols	Customer Service		
Z3	Encryption	Global IP address	packet	Twistted pair	Prepaid cash card		
Z4	Cyphertext	Encryption	Behaviour	Fibre optic	E-clearing house		
Z5	Connection points	Data Storage	Wireless	Magnetic cheque	Server side		
Z6							
Z7							

LEVEL 4 - Integrate Risk

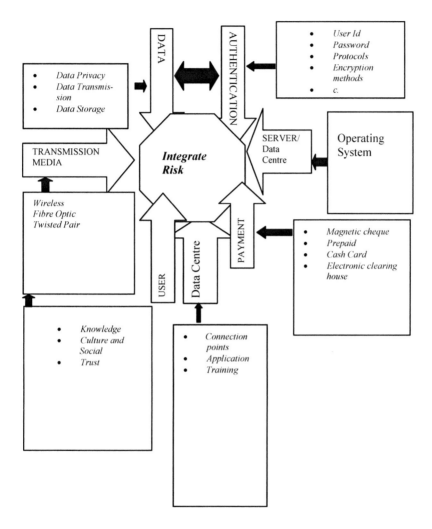

LEVEL 5 - Audit Risk

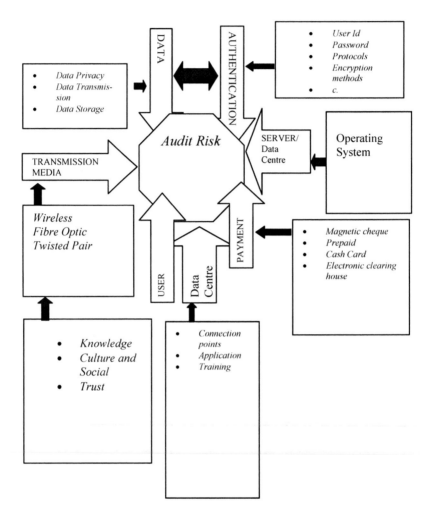

LEVEL 6 - (RISG) Risk Identification Solution Grid

	Z1	Z2	Z3	Z4	Z5	Z6	Z7
Z1	knowledge	skill	configuration	Applications	Operating System		
Z2	Training	Trust	User ID	Protocols	Customer Service		
Z3	Encryption	Global IP address	packet	Twistted pair	Prepaid cash card		
Z4	Cyphertext	Encryption	Behaviour	Fibre optic	E-clearing house		
Z5	Connection points	Data Storage	Wireless	Magnetic cheque	Server side		
Z6							
Z7							

SOLUTIONS

9.6   SSTM Results and Analysis

Risk Access Spots (RAS) are mainly gathered from the questionnaire feed-back. The number one top priority is *knowledge*. 81% expressed their regret for not having enough knowledge to access the Internet. Also 33% of the respondents outside Sudan do not have online banking accounts for the same reason. The results from SSTM highlight knowledge and computer literacy as hurdles which need to be overcome if an e-payment system is to be successful in Sudan.

Skill and *Training* are connected in many ways. For example, you can not improve skill unless you have good training. Issues such as training and skill are critical to developing economies. For instance skills set in UNIX, Netware, Windows, and CISCO router were low amongst developing economies as compared to advanced economies Williams (2004).

These facts stress the need for training by skilled instructors with the appropriate facilities to improve the skills of employees and therefore make them feel confident when they deal with the new system or solve problems connected to it.

Another important RAS was "trust" as it was the main reason given for not having a bank account. One of the respondents expressed his mistrust by saying:" *I couldn't get cash out of my account because the bank didn't have enough liquidity at that time*". Due to these reasons they prefer to keep their money in an accessible place, such as at home, where they can get it when ever they want it.

9.7   Findings

The findings of this study were extracted from risk assessment using data from interviews, questionnaires distributed to Sudanese citizens both inside and out side Sudan.

At Level 6 of SSTM or RISG, the Risk Access Spots are prioritised. The analysis of the findings of this level demonstrate a high Risk from Users, as all Risk Access Spots highlighted under User are between Z1, and Z3. This indicates the need for investing in training and education. Also the analysis highlighted the following points.

- The Central Bank of Sudan is working hard to improve the banking system and to computerise the banking system, but unfortunately the infrastructure is not yet ready to welcome these changes.
- The Central Bank of Sudan is trying to over come some of the infrastructure related obstacles, like using UPS in case of power failure.
- The digital divide between Sudan and other advanced countries is huge as observed in this study.
- There is mistrust among customers with regards to the banking system; due to lack of knowledge of the system.
- The cultural and social beliefs often serve as barriers to change for stakeholders.

9.8   Recommendations Made to Stakeholders from the Study

- More attention needs to be given to basic infrastructural services such as electricity and communications. Although the Sudanese Telecommunication Company (Sudatel) is doing very well, the prices of its services are still high.
- Businesses and profitable organisations should be encouraged to make more use of the banking system, for example they can pay their employees salary, or accept customers bill payments by direct debit.
- Enforce and introduce computer literacy in earlier education stages, and pay more attention to computer literacy in general.
- Make use of scientific studies from advanced economies, and give more support to scientists and scientific researches.
- Use oil revenues to invest in people by encouraging innovation through funding research and supporting distinguished students.
- Promoting knowledge by opening public libraries and providing less expensive public Internet access.
- Promote the banking industry by helping individuals to open bank accounts, for example commercial banks can reduce the minimum deposit required to open an account, or introduce new schemes that suit people with less income.
- Assess the international directives that govern both banking systems and ICT, and produce laws that are suited to the case of Sudan.

- Promoting technology by arranging conferences and setting up societies that encourage experts from advanced economies to get involved in the Sudan ICT and business logic agenda.
- Direct all official and governmental financial transactions to go through the banking sector.
- Provide periodical training sessions to help to Keep the technical employees up to date with technology, also insist on getting them certified.

9.9   Summary

Chapter 9 presented a simulation of SSTM using 4 case scenarios. The objective of the simulations was to assess the reliability and trustworthiness of the model. It assessed security risk in Online Business Security for heterogeneous and hetero-standard systems with respect to communication networks using Monte Carlo method. The simulations addressed issues with respect to how security was assessed in organisations which had both local and global network infrastructure, how such risks threatened the confidentiality, integrity and availability of information services. Using SSTM probability of risk was calculated to determine seriousness of risk.

Chapter 10

Discussions

Online Business is driven by different systems. The systems consist of commercial activities, legal frameworks, security technologies, information system standards and policies as well as risk management models for assessing and determining strategies for security risk assessment and mitigation.

This book provided an overview of commercial activities and processes in Online Business. It gave an insight of commercial activities associated with Internet based services, Cash points, Electronic Point of Sale (EPOS) cash register and Telephone Banking activities. The role of payment systems and gateways in Online Business was discussed. Online Business Systems and technologies which drive electronic business and commerce have always been subjected to attacks. This is due to vulnerabilities associated with these systems and technologies. Human vulnerability is likely to become a permanent security issue so far as Online Business activities remain consumer driven.

The processes common to all these commercial activities include authentication, authorisation and answerability of transactions and activities in Online based systems. Risk and security solution models on the market have primarily focused on a third party security model paradigm instead of distributed security model paradigm. Third party security models and systems aim to protect personal and financial welfare of consumers. In an attempt to achieve this objective, the systems rather subject legitimate consumers to unnecessary security checks and verification processes. Third party security models are mono-directional. Thus, they attempt to authenticate, authorise and answer the request of the consumer on the basis of false negative. False negative means that the model checks whether answers in response to security questions from the consumer matches with data stored about the consumer. This has led to attackers and fraudsters being able to clone counterfeits of legitimate profiles of consumers. The model barely tracks non authentic marks of an attacker or a fraudster. The information kept about the consumer is usually stored for too long. Empirical studies conducted confirm this assertion. At present mobile phone service providers have large databases that stores consumer personal details. The information in these databases is sometimes traded among service providers for marketing purposes without due regard to consumers legal rights. There are also people in these businesses who deliberately sell the information in the databases. This is tantamount to a criminal offence. Poor control and monitoring systems make it easier to clone any data set for the purposes of fraudulent activities leading to identity theft.

A distributed security risk model such as the SSTM builds a profile of security risk zones of Online Business Systems usually exploited by criminals. This approach leads to a counter attack on the criminal. This approach is more effective than indirect focusing on legitimate activities of a consumer for authentication, authorisation and approval of transactions made by the consumer. It is not an easy cut solution model. Data matching to an extent is a primitive approach to security risk management. There is over emphasis on consumer verification. This approach has made attacks such as identity fraud quite successful.

The role of software agents in payment systems and online marketing and sales seem to be on the ascendancy. The nature of software agents as reviewed in chapter 1 suggests the need to have systems that verify trustworthiness.

The legislative functions of businesses do seem to be docile and ineffective. There are numerous cases of data protection violations by service providers which have not been tracked by third party organisations and law enforcement agencies. Different countries have their legal systems and issues with respect to Online transactions that affect security management.

Online Business Systems are both Heterogeneous and Hetero-standard. The term "Heterogeneous system" in lay term refers to two or more computers or communication networks services by different vendors. These vendors have the capability to operate and communicate using different hardware and software. "Hetero-standard system" refers to communication networks governed by different security or quality standards

There are standards and protocols that govern these technologies. Protocols, Standards and technologies such as SET, SSL and IPSEC form common security technologies adopted by Online Businesses. Crypto-systems PPP, CHAP and Kerberos contribute to authentication in Online Business. In order for authentication to be successful, key questions such as; are we dealing with the right customer? Does the debit/credit card belong to this person? should be satisfactorily answered.

Risk Access Spots (RAS) common to communication networks identified and discussed in this book were Transmission media (Cables, Electromagnetic Spectrum (EMS)), Service Providers (IP addresses, port and port numbers, computer and network servers), MAC address and the Human activity system. There was review of two common servers, the apache and tomcat servers. There was detail analysis of risks access spots associated with operating system software.

A pedagogical view of methods used by hackers and crackers to exploit network vulnerabilities in Online Business Systems was discussed. The attacks exploited vulnerabilities such as transmission media (Wired and Wireless spectrum, Service Access Points (SAP), Routing Table & IP address, Port and Port number, MAC address, Server, User Profiles, Cyphertext and Crypto-systems and Operating Systems. The defence and management strategies for handling these attacks on a communication network supporting Online Business has been presented in chapters 4, 7, 8 and 9. Chapter 4 reviewed existing security technologies and methods, while chapters 7 and 8 discussed security risk models. Chapter proposed SSTM as a more secure and robust model for analysing risk and threats in Online Business Systems.

Common methods of attacks covered were Brute Force, Traffic Analysis using tools such as Snort, Profiling, Scavenging, Spoofing (Web, DNS, IP), Stealth Attacks, Denial of Service (DOS) (SYN Flood, Smurf, TCP ACK Flooding etc), Distributed Denial of Service (DDOS), Malware propagation (Worms, Viruses, Bots, Spyware) using mobile codes, Man in the Middle, Replay, TCP Session Hijacking, ARP, (Address Resolution Protocol) pollution, IP Fragmentation, Replay, TCP Session Hijacking, Password conjecture and guesswork, Backdoor, Ping, Permutation analysis and exhaustive key search. Software tools and utility computer programs used by hackers to exploit vulnerabilities were discussed.

SSTM highlights the fact that there are risk access spots that need to be identified in the development process of such systems. It also suggests the need to determine perceived risk and actual risk. Although the risks identified are of critical importance to such systems, the risk areas could evolve or change. The underlying mathematical model is applied to electronic business cases with regards to on-line banking and results presented in chapter 9.

Concepts and notations described comprised, risk, (r), RAS (Risk Access Spots) and Zones. Zones can be local or global. They are graded as 1, 2 and 3 meaning low, medium and high levels. RIG (Risk Identification Grid) for integrating risk extracted during risk assessment. Factors essential to synchronization process were outlined. These include time, event and attack, as well as the Zone. RISG (Risk Identification and Solutions Grid) a tabulation of recommended solutions for the security risk problem identified in RIG was also presented. There is emphasis on guidelines for implementing SSTM.

10.1   Bibliography and References

(A consice introduction). Westview Press. 107,2000. 2004.
A new approach for assessing the maturity of information security
Accessed (06/08/04).

Adshead A (2001) Lloyd's to save £4m with VoIP network, Network

Althos (2001) Publishing Inc., ISBN: 0-9742787-7-7.
and Voice compression, 2001.

Arreymbi J, Williams (2006) EEMA presentation on Cybertribes, 16th May,
Green Park Reading UK.

Atkinson Ashley Atkinson, Magazine Director, Keycom.

Bregman (2001) Bregman David, Reality check on VoIP (Internet

Buchman DH (1994) Risk Analysis – some practical suggestions

Bussgang J.J and Spar D (1996) Harvard Business Review. Means of
Exchange and Security enforcement. Pg. 129-131, 131-132

Chapman & Ward (1997) Project Risk Management. Wiley: Chichester.

Chartrand, Mark R (2004) Satellite Communication for the non-specialist

Chen T (2004) "Intrusion detection for viruses and worms," in IEC Annual
Review of Communications, vol. 57.

Cisco (2000) Cisco Systems Inc., VoIP Today, 2000.CiscoPress

Collins (2001) Daniel Collins "Carrier Grade Voice Over IP"

Databeam (2004) A Primer on the H.323 Series Standard version 2

Databeam, www.databeam.com/h323/h323primer.html

Davidson (2000) J Davidson, J Peters "Voice over IP fundamentals"

Dean Tamara (2003) Guide to Telecommunication Technology Deception,
Fraud

Deremiak EL and Boreman GD (1996) Infrared Detectors and Systems

Dixon M, Robert McCorquodate. Cases and Materials on international law, Blackstone Press Limited. 306, 138, 276

Electro-technical conference, MELECON, V1, P250 – 254. February 2003, P304 – 310.

Ferrie P and Perriot F (2004), Virus Analysis 2, Symantec Security for Internet Telephony, 2000.

Glasson B, Doug Vogel, Peter Bots and Jay Nunmaker. Glenn et al (1999) Wireless Information Technology for the 21st Century group. Missouri research and education network

Gu X, Dodds SJ (2006) Open Source Publication on Communication Networks and electornic Security. Journal for ICT security synergy in advanced and developing economies Volume 1

Halsall (2001) Fred Halsall "Multimedia Communications" Pearson

Handley et al (2000) SIP: Session Initiation Protocol IETF, Ineternet draft,

Harrison G (2004) Videonetworks Network Design, 23rd march, 2004.

Harte L (2003) Introduction to IP Telephony. Copyright 2003

Hignera & Haines (1996), Software Risk Management. Technical Report, Software Engineering Institute, Pittsburgh, PA, USA

IBM(2004) Global security KIT, SSL introduction and ikeyman user's improvement of VoIP applications. Proceedings of the Mediterranean Information Systems and technology in the international office of the future. Chapman & Hall. 30, 31, 34

James M (2004) Voice over IP (How IT works), Computer Shopper

Jones R (1997). Business and Technology Journal. Net can't catch Cyber criminals Journal

Keen P, Mackintosh R (2001)The Freedom Economy. Gaining the M-commerce Edge in the Era of the Wireless Internet

Koistinen T (1998) IP Telephony. Nokia Communications

Kos, Klepec, Tomaziac (2002) "Techniques for Performance

Krishnamoorthy V (2001) "The Importance of QoS in Broadband

Lee W, Mcknight, Lehr W, Clark D (2001) "Internet Telephony" Copyright

Levi W (2004) Contemporary international law
magazine, November 2004, P4.

Mehta P, Udani S (2001) Overview of Voice over IP Technical report

Minoli D, Minoli E (1998) "Delivery Voice over IP Networks"

Mirecki F (2002) VoIP Unified Messaging, Technology seminar

Morgan EB (2004) A white Paper on Voice Over IP Packet,
MS-CIS-01-31.

Musaj (2006) A holistic definition of IT Security
Information Systems Control (ISACA) Journal volume 3

Networks and Electronic Security. Journal for ICT Security.
networks at risk, Network News News, 13 December 2001

NIST (2002) 27 March, technology administration US department
NIST lab of commerce

Oni (2001) "The Guide to IP Telephony" ONI(2001).

Onwubiko C (2006) Open Source publication on Communication Networks
and Electronic Security Volume 1– Journal for ICT security synergy in
advanced and developing economies

Oslon D (2002) Voice over IP: Technical issues, Strategic technology P20.

Project Management Institute (1996) A Guide To Project Management
Body Of Knowledge (PMBOK), Project Institute, Newton Square, PA, USA

Protocol (2004) Protocols, Technical Paper on Protocols

Reitter, Jorg Reitter(2004) "Net Telephony For All" Linux Magazine,
Response, USA

Richardson J (2004) Technical Extracts, Keycom.

Robinson NE (2005) Using GIS Tool to assess the vulnerability of the internet. Securing Electronic Business Processes, Vieweg

Rogers G (2001) Rogers Gary, A Gateway from old to the New, Sonus

Rogerson S (1997) Institute for the management of information systems (IMIS) journal. ETHIcol. march 1997. 21

Saleh Alaboodi Saad (2006) Information Systems Control (ISACA) Journal Volume 3.

Schulzrinne H, Rosenberg J (2000) A comparison of SIP and H323

Singleton TW (2006) COBIT - A Key to success as an ICT auditor, Information Systems Control Journal

Shaneck M. An Overview of Buffer Overflow Vulnerabilities and Internet

Smart Nigel (2003) Cryptography: An introduction. McGraw-Hill

Smith K, Brushteyn D (2004) A Paper on Internet Telephony

Stallings W(2003) Network Security Essentials. Pearson

Steven J et al (1997) JAVA security model, Sun Micro Systems 1996/97

Symantec (2004) Internet Security Threat Report, Trends for January 1, 2004 – June 30, 2004, Symantec, Volume VI

Telogy Networks. www.telogy.com accessed (06/08/04).

Vittore V (2003) Making the case for IP Telephony, Telephony, v244, n4,

Williams (1995) A classified bibliography of recent research relating to project risk management European Journal Of Operational research 85: 18-38.

Williams G (2003/4) Synchronizing E-Security Kluwer Academic Publishers,

Woabank (2000) Research Paper, Butler Group (Research and

Wong H, C, Sycara K (1999) "Adding security and trust to Multi-Agent

Additional Bibliography

1. Alberts, Christopher J; Belmens, Sandra G; Rethia, Richard D, & Wilson, William R. Operationally Critical Threat, Asset, and Vulnerability Evaluation (OCTAVE) Framework version 1.0 (CMU/SE 1-99-JR-017), Pittsburgh, PA: Software Engineering Institute, Carnegie Mellon University, June 1999.

2. National Security Telecommunications and Information Systems Security Committee. Index of National Security Telecommunications Information Systems Security issuances (NSTSS1 No. 4014) Ft. Mead, MD: NSTISSC secretariat Jan. 1998

3. Howard, John D & Longstaff, Thomas A. A common language for computer security incidents (SAND 98 -8667). Albuquerque, NM: Sandia National Laboratories 1998

4. Hatt, Aurthur E; Bosworth, Seymour; Hoyt Douglas B. Computer Security Handbook, 3rd Edition. New York, NY: John Wiley & Sons, Inc 1995

5. Parker, Donn B. Fighting Computer Crime. New York, NY: John Wiley & Sons, Inc 1998

Internet Publications and web resources

Worms, University of Minnesota, 2003
www.cis.upenn.edu/~kellyann/papes/iphone.html.Accessed (05/08/04).
www.protocols.com/pbook/voip.htm accessed (05/08/04).

Published Advisories (2003), Analysis: Blaster Worm, eEye Digital Security,
http://www.eeye.com/html/Research/Advisories/AL20030811.html

Newsham T (2000), Format string attacks, Guardent, Inc. http://downloads.securityfocus.com/library/Format String.pdf

Atstake.com, Mac OS X pppd Format String Vulnerability,
http://www.atstake.com/research/advisories/2004/a022304-1.txt

Red Hat Linux, Updated CUPS packages fix denial of service attack,
http://www.redhat.com/support/errata/RHSA-2003171.html

Red Hat, RHSA-2004:259,
http://www.redhat.com/support/errata/RHSA-2004-259.html

Microsoft, MS04-011,
http://www.microsoft.com/technet/security/bulletin/MS04-011.mspx

Bugtraq,Security,
http://archives.neohapsis.com/archives/vendor/20003/0002.html
http://marc.theaimsgroup.com/?l=bugtraq&m=101318944130790&w=2

ByteRage (2001) Windows MS-DOS Device Name DoS vulnerabilities,
http://archives.neohapsis.com/archives/bugtraq/2001-07/0086.html

Red Hat (2003), Updated Kerberos packages fix vulnerability in ftp client,
http://www.redhat.com/support/errata/RHSA-2003-020.html

ISS X-Force, rlogin-froot(104),
http://xforce.iss.net/static/104.php

Full-Disclosure, 20040413 Microsoft Help and Support Centre argument
injection vulnerability,

http://lists.netsys.com/pipermail/full-isclosure/2004April/020065.html

Counterpane(2002), Internet Security, Security Alert: New Pattern in IIS,
18 June 2002,
http://www.counterpane.com/alert-iispattern.html
Accessed 03/05/05

CVE Vulnerability Search Engine,
http://icat.nist.gov/icat.cfm?cvename=CAN-2001-1238

SS X-Force, firewall-rst-fingerprint(8738),
http://www.iss.net/security_center/static/8738.php

Bugtraq, 2004-0020,
http://marc.theaimsgroup.com/?l=bugtraq&m=108213675028441&w=2

CVE Vulnerability Search Engine,
http://icat.nist.gov/icat.cfm?cvename=CAN-2004-0123

Gadue D J(2004), Using Proactive Depth in Defence to Ease Patch
Management Problems, GSEC Practical Assignment.

RedHat, RHSA-2001:148-09,
http://www.redhat.com/support/errata/RHSA-2001-148.html

CVE Vulnerability Search Engine,
http://icat.nist.gov/icat.cfm?cvename=CAN-2001-0978

CVE Vulnerability Search Engine,
http://icat.nist.gov/icat.cfm?cvename=CAN-2004-0427
Accessed 20/04/06

Microsoft TechNet, MS98-017,
http://www.microsoft.com/technet/security/bulletin/ms98-017.asp
Accessed 20/04/05

ISS X-Force, tcp-mss-dos,
http://xforce.iss.net/static/6824.php
Accessed 05/10/06

ISSX-Force,macos-opentransport-dos(3752),
http://xforce.iss.net/static/3752.php
Accessed 12/01/05

Red Hat Linux, Updated 2.4 kernel fixes vulnerabilities and driver bugs,
http://www.redhat.com/support/errata/RHSA-2003-187.html
Accessed 01/04/04

The Aims Group, NetScreen ScreenOS 2.6 Subject to Trust Interface DoS,
http://marc.theaimsgroup.com/?l=bugtraq&m=101258281818524&w=2:
Accessed 20/04/05

CVE Vulnerability Search Engine,
http://icat.nist.gov/icat.cfm?cvename=CVE-2000-0979

Symantec Virus Encyclopedia, W32.Opaserv.Worm,
http://securityresponse.symantec.com/avcen-
er/venc/data/w32.opaserv.worm.html : Accessed 10/02/2007

AtStake.com, Ethernet frame padding information leakage,
http://www.atstake.com/research/advisories/2003/a010603-1.txt

ISS X-Force, tcp-mss-dos, http://xforce.iss.net/static/6824.php

Steven M. Christey, Vulnerability Auditing Checklist,
2004, http://www.mail-archive.com/sc-l@securecoding.org/msg00230.html

Microsoft Corporation (2005) 'VPN Architecture' (online)
Accessed 24th February 2005.
http://www.microsoft.com/resources/documentation/WindowsServ/2003/all/
techref/enus/Default.asp?url=/Resources/Documentation/windowsserv/2003/
all/techref/en-us/w2k3tr_vpn_how.asp

Index

Printed in the United Kingdom
by Lightning Source UK Ltd.
135058UK00002B/184/A